Table of Contents

New Testament

Matthew..3

Mark..12

Luke..21

John..29

Acts...45

Romans...54

1 Corinthians..60

2 Corinthians..66

Galatians...70

Ephesians...73

Philippians..76

Colossians..78

1 Thessalonians...................................80

2 Thessalonians...................................82

1 Timothy..84

2 Timothy..87

Titus..90

Philemon...92

Hebrews..93

James...98

1 Peter...101

2 Peter...103

1 John...105

2 John...107

3 John...107

Jude...108

Revelation...109

Intro

This book serves as a comprehensive chapter by chapter guide to The New Testament. It can be used for the modern reader seeking insight and clarity. Whether someone is the new to the New Testament or just looking to deepen understanding, this guide aims to illuminate the timeless wisdom and messages from the books in the Bible in a clear, accessible way. It begins with the four gospels, exploring the life and teachings of Jesus. The first two gospels Matthew and Mark are examined chapter by chapter, providing a detailed walkthrough of their texts. For the gospels of Luke and John, the focus shifts slightly. Rather than repeating what has already been covered, this guide highlights only the passages unique in their gospel. This approach allows readers to appreciate the distinctive elements and fresh insights each gospel brings to the story of Jesus, without exceeding repetitive verses. Not that there is anything wrong with repetitive parallel verses, this is just a guide to understand the uniqueness of each gospel.

This is not official doctrine or a translation, it is a summarized version of scripture. The New Testament has approximately one hundred and eighty thousand words. The message of The New Testament is to spread the good news of Jesus.

The writers of the first manuscripts of the gospels knew and spoke to the witnesses of Jesus' closest followers, companions, disciples, and apostles. This is not some book somebody wrote at some point in time, it is recorded history and sixty-six books written over thousands of years by over forty authors in multiple languages on multiple continents. Early manuscripts of the gospels and letters ended up in different continents telling the same story of what happened, and not contradicting each other. The New Testament today consists of the same messages that were read during the first four centuries of its existence. The official full New Testament did not appear earlier is because it was individual letters, gospels, old and new testament books, written on scrolls. When Christianity became decriminalized in the Roman empire in the third century, the codex format for the Bible became more practical and durable. Codex Sinaiticus and Codex Vaticanus is from the fourth century, P52 and P66 is from the second or early third century. Codex Vaticanus, Codex Sinaiticus, and Papyrus P66 are independent manuscripts with notable textual and formatting differences, but the teachings of Jesus remain the same today as then.

The New Testament starts out by introducing the life and teachings of Jesus four different times, showing all the different testimonies. The story is so complex it takes multiple times to grasp the ideas Jesus speaks of, not even his own disciples understood what he was saying at first. Jesus' message of forgiveness, compassion, and loving enemies was something never seen before in history. The audiences for each gospel is different, with Matthew writing to more of a Jewish audience and Mark to more of a gentile, non-Jewish audience. Gospel of Luke was written with a Greek speaking gentile audience in mind, and gospel of John targeting a broad audience of both Jewish and gentile believers.

Matthew

Matthew the apostle and tax collector is attributed with this gospel. Jesus is here to bring salvation to the ends of the earth. This gospel shows that God always keeps his divine promises through the life, death, and resurrection of Christ. Jesus is represented like Moses; he is the prophesied one who is greater than Moses. He will save people from sin, preach, and teach. The gospel is written in sections of Jesus' life and teachings, delivering a new covenant. Jesus is referred to as Immanuel, a name which translates to "God with us." At the end, Jesus sends his followers into the world with a promise that he is with them.

In chapter 1, it opens with a genealogy tracing Jesus Christ's ancestry back to Abraham and David. There are forty-two generations between Abraham and Jesus. This genealogy is structured in three groups of fourteen generations. The first section is from Abraham to King David, the next fourteen generations are from King David to Babylonian exile, and the last fourteen are from the exile to the birth Jesus Christ. The next part of the chapter tells of Jesus' miraculous birth. Jesus' mother Mary had promised to be married to Joseph, but before they came together she was found to be pregnant through the holy spirit. Joseph was upset and could not believe it at first. He did not want to embarrass Mary or expose her to be a public disgrace. The first thought on his mind was to just divorce her quietly. After he considered these things, an angel of the lord appeared to him in a dream and said, "Joseph, son of David, do not be afraid to take Mary home as your wife, because what is conceived in her is from the holy spirit. She will give birth to a son, and you are to give him the name Jesus." Joseph is told that he will save his people from their sins. Joseph woke up from the dream and he did what the angel of the lord commanded. He took Mary home as his wife, and did not consummate until after she gave birth. Joseph gave him the name Jesus. In Isaiah seven-fourteen, the prophecy is fulfilled saying a virgin will conceive and give birth to a son, and will call him Immanuel.

In chapter 2, King Herod was disturbed to hear news that the messiah and king of the Jews had been born in Bethlehem. Herod had an ego, and his title was king of the Jews, not somebody else. He called on some men named Magi to go to Bethlehem and search carefully for this child. These men Herod sent were warned in a dream not to go back to him. The Magi saw the child with his mother Mary, and they bowed down and worshipped him. After these men were warned in a dream, they took a different route back to their countries. The angel of the lord appeared to Joseph again and warned him to take the child and Mary to escape to Egypt. The angel told Joseph that Herod was going to search for the child and kill him. Joseph got up and took the child and mother during the night and left for Egypt, where he stayed until the death of Herod. When Herod heard that the Magi outwitted him, he was furious and gave orders to kill all the boys in Bethlehem who were two years old and under. This is what the prophet Jeremiah prophesied and now fulfilled, a prophecy about a time where God brings a new covenant and a women named Rachel weeping for her children. After Herod died, the angel of the lord appeared to Joseph again in a dream and told him to get up and take the child and his mother to Israel, the ones trying to take the child are dead. They went to a town called Nazareth.

In chapter 3, John the Baptist baptizes Jesus. John was reluctant to baptize Jesus because he knew Jesus was sinless and perfect, so John felt unworthy and thought it should be the other way around of Jesus baptizing him. After an initial hesitation, John complied because Jesus said it must be done to fulfill righteousness. As soon as Jesus was baptized, heaven was opened and the spirit of God descended like a dove. A voice from heaven said this is my Son, whom I love; with him I am well pleased.

In chapter 4, Jesus is tested in the wilderness. After fasting forty days and forty nights, he was hungry. Satan the accuser and tempter came to him in the desert and said if he is really the son of God, for him to turn these stones into bread. Jesus replied and said man shall not live on bread alone, but on every word that comes from the mouth of God. Then the devil took Jesus to the holy city and had him stand on the highest point of the temple and tells him to throw himself down and jump, and that if he is the son of God, then surely angels will lift him up. Jesus replied and told him it is written to not put the Lord your God to the test. The devil made one last attempt and showed Jesus all the kingdoms of the world and their greatness. The devil said if he just bowed down and worshipped him, he would give all this. Jesus told Satan to get away from him. It says to worship the Lord God, and serve him only. In the next part of the chapter, Jesus begins to preach. Following John's arrest, Jesus leaves Nazareth to live in Capernaum. This move fulfills another prophecy from Isaiah. Jesus says to repent, for the kingdom of heaven has come near. Jesus calls his first disciples. He saw two brothers, Simon-Peter and Andrew. They were fisherman. They leave their nets and follow him. Then Jesus calls James and John, who also leave their boat to follow. Jesus healed the sick, he went throughout Galilee, teaching in their synagogues, proclaiming the good news of the kingdom, and healing every disease and sickness among the people. News about him spread all over. People came to Jesus bringing others who were ill and had various diseases, suffering severe pain, demon-possessed, those having seizures, and the paralyzed. Jesus healed them. Large crowds followed Jesus in Galilee, Jerusalem, Judea, and more.

In chapter 5, The Sermon on the Mount is introduced. When Jesus saw crowds, he went up on a mountainside and sat down. His disciples came to him, and he began to teach them. Jesus introduces the beatitudes, where he sends out blessings on the mount. Jesus is establishing a new covenant where salvation is attainable, and hearts are open. Jesus stated, blessed are the poor in spirit, for their kingdom is in heaven. Blessed is those who mourn, for they will be comforted. Blessed is the meek, for they will inherit the earth. Blessed is those who hunger and thirst for righteousness, they will be filled. Blessed is the merciful, for they will be shown mercy. Blessed is the pure in heart, they will see God. Blessed are the peacemakers; they will be called the children of God. Blessed is those who have been persecuted wrongly while fighting for righteousness, theirs is the kingdom of heaven. He says when people insult you, persecute you, and falsely say all kinds of evil against you because of him, rejoice and be glad, because great is the reward in heaven. Same goes for the prophets before them who died and were persecuted in the name of the Lord.

Jesus uses metaphors of salt and light to describe the influence of his followers in the world. He tells them to maintain their saltiness and let their light shine before others through good deeds, so that people may glorify God. Then Jesus talks about the laws and former prophets. He tells the people he is not here to abolish the laws of Moses; he has come to fulfill them. He is here to fulfill God's promises of a savior to restore humanity and give new teachings, a new covenant. At the end of chapter five up until chapter seven, it goes into detail about sin and life lessons. He teaches them the lord's prayer. Jesus gives specific teachings on each topic such as murder, adultery, divorce, oaths, eye for an eye, loving enemies, giving to the needy, prayer, fasting, treasures in heaven, not to worry, judging others, ask seek knock, true and false prophets and disciples, the wise and foolish.

In chapter 8, Jesus reminds them of the commitment necessary for discipleship. It also provides a series of miracles displaying Jesus' authority over sickness, nature, and spiritual forces. When Jesus was walking down the mountainside with large crowds following him, a man with leprosy came and knelt before him and asked Jesus to make him clean, if the lord is willing. Jesus said he is willing and simply said for the man to be clean, and the man was immediately cleansed. Then Jesus told him to go show himself to the priest and offer the gift Moses commanded, as testimony to them. After that, a centurion man approached Jesus and told him about a servant who is paralyzed and suffering terribly. Jesus said to him "Shall I come heal him?" The Centurion man humbled himself and replied by saying, "Lord, I do not deserve to have you come under my roof." Jesus healed the man's servant from a distance. After that, Jesus heals Peter's mother-in-law at Peter's house, touching her hand, and the fever leaves her. When the evening came, many who were demon possessed came to Jesus, and he drove out the spirits with a word and healed the sick. Jesus gives a warning to anyone who follows him. It comes at a cost like not having a place to lay their head and rest. They will be subject to prosecution. Jesus already knows that the leaders would see him as a threat and reject him, therefore rejecting his followers too. As Jesus and his disciples cross the Sea of Galilee, a violent storm arises. Jesus calms the storm and the men. He rebuked the winds and waves, and it was suddenly calm. This shocked his disciples and showed his authority over nature. Then he saw two demon-possessed men, and they recognized Jesus' authority; they begged if their spirits can be moved to the den of pigs over there. Jesus said go and the demons were cast from the men into the animals.

In chapter 9, it gives people a picture of Jesus' divinity and authority. His miracles confirm his divinity, while his teachings redefine religious practices. It starts out with Jesus forgiving and healing a paralytic brought by his friends. Jesus approaches Matthew, a tax collector who was called upon to follow Jesus. The lord wants mercy, not sacrifice. The messiah is here to save all the sinners, not just the righteous. The disciples ask about fasting. Jesus heals a bleeding woman and restores a girl to life. He restored the blind and the deaf. Jesus traveled among all the cities and villages, teaching in their synagogues, announcing the good news of the kingdom, and healing every disease and every sickness. When Jesus saw the crowds, he had compassion for them because they were troubled and helpless, like sheep without a shepherd.

In chapter 10, Jesus calls his twelve disciples and gives them authority over unclean spirits and to heal. The disciples will be given special authority so they can establish God's new kingdom and spread the word. Jesus sends the disciples out with specific instructions, they are to go to the lost sheep of Israel, proclaim the kingdom of heaven, heal the sick, raise the dead, cleanse the lepers, and cast out demons. Jesus warns his disciples they will be persecuted in the lord's name. Jesus says that everyone will hate them on account of his holy name. But whoever stands firm until the end will be saved. Their testimonies will be remembered, and their names will be preserved until his return. Jesus reassures the disciples not to fear those who can only kill the body but cannot kill the soul, instructing them instead to fear God who can destroy both soul and body. He reassures them of their value and worth. Jesus explains that his message will cause divisions within households. He calls for wholehearted commitment from his disciples, who must be ready to take up the cross and follow him. There will be a reward for the faithful.

In chapters 11, it shows the response to Jesus from the people. There are some who accept he is the messiah, and others who fail to repent such as the cities of Bethsaida, Capernaum and Chorazin. Woe to the unrepentant cities. John the Baptist gets imprisoned and faces difficulties. The disciples confirm the miracles of Jesus, and John realizes that Jesus is the messiah he is supposed to pave the way for. Jesus praises John's ministry and John accepts his role as a prophet. Jesus offers salvation and rest to the weary and burdened, and also addresses the consequences of doubt and unrepentance. The Father is revealed in the son, all things have been committed to the son through the Father.

In chapter 12, it teaches about the authority of Jesus, and the importance of faith and compassion. The pharisees challenge Jesus and his disciples for their actions on the sabbath, saying plucking grain on sabbath is unlawful. Jesus declares himself lord of the sabbath and says it is more important to have compassion and mercy, rather than trying to strictly adhere to religious rules. After that he went into their synagogue and there was a man with a shriveled hand, Jesus heals the hand and the pharisees question whether it is lawful to heal on the sabbath. The pharisees start plotting how they are going to kill him. It gives a warning against blaspheming the holy spirit, which in other words is a person with a hardened heart that refuses to see truth despite miracles right in front of their eyes. Jesus uses an analogy of a tree and its fruit, explaining someone's words reveal their heart. People will be judged on the day of judgement for the careless words they use, especially if it is against the holy spirit. A teacher of law requests a sign, but Jesus refuses and promises the sign of Jonah. Believers who follow the will of the Father are connected through faith in Jesus, which transcends blood relationships.

In chapter 13, it describes many parables such as the parable of the Sower, the parable of the weeds, the parable of the mustard seed and the yeast, the parable of the hidden treasure and the pearl, and the parable of the net. I will describe each parable in one sentence. The parable of the Sower explains how people react to the gospel, some receive it, and others reject it. The parable of the weeds symbolizes the coexistence of good and evil until the final judgment. The parable of the mustard seed symbolizes God's future kingdom that expands to ends of the earth they cannot even imagine. The parable of the hidden treasure and the pearl, these symbolize the value of the kingdom of heaven, which is worth giving up everything to possess. The parable of the net, which describes a kingdom where there is a final judgement of souls, the good and bad souls will be separated and judged at the end of the age.

In Chapter 14, King Herod executed John the Baptist. John's head was brought on a platter and given to a girl, who carried it to her mother. John's disciples take his body and bury it. Crowds follow Jesus around and there was five thousand people. Jesus miraculously multiplies five loaves and two fish into enough food to feed all of them. After feeding the people, Jesus sent the disciples across the sea, and he starts praying alone. Jesus walked on water and when Peter tried, he sunk, Jesus grabbed him. Jesus told Peter he would not have fell if he had put more confidence in his faith.

In chapter 15, Jesus and his disciples get accused of breaking tradition by not washing hands before eating. Jesus counters them by pointing out the pharisees hypocrisy, they neglect God's commandments for human tradition. Jesus explained that what defiles a person comes from the heart, not from what they eat. After that, Jesus does more healing, he casts out the demon of a possessed Canaanite women. Then the lord continues to heal and feed thousands of people at a time by the sea of Galilee.

In chapter 16, Jesus talks about his death and what to expect. Peter confesses that Jesus is the messiah and Christ, the son of the living God. Jesus blesses Peter, saying this knowledge was revealed by God, and predicts the future establishment of his church with Peter playing a significant role. Jesus is followed by thousands of people, both Jew and gentile. They are inspired and encouraged by him, but the religious leaders are threated. Jesus is here to establish God's kingdom and spirit to all nations. In this new kingdom, they gain honor for serving and helping others. Jesus knew that he would be sentenced to death, so he gathered his closest disciples and gave them the knowledge of what is to come. Jesus begins to prepare his disciples for his upcoming suffering, death, and resurrection. Jesus shows his disciples that they may take a similar fate as the cost of discipleship. Jesus tells them whoever wants to be his disciple must deny themselves and take up their cross and follow him. He asks, what good is the whole world if one must forfeit their soul. Jesus was trying to explain to the disciples that God's kingdom over earth was going to be established through his death, it will fulfill Old Testament prophecy. The disciples were confused at some ideas and ask who then can be saved, to which Jesus responds that with God all things are possible.

In chapter 17, it focuses on the transfiguration of Jesus, which is revealed to Peter, James, and John. This showed that Jesus was greater than the prophets and the law. Jesus was transformed and God's voice came out of the clouds saying that this is his son who he loves. Moses and Elijah appeared conversing with Jesus, and Peter asked if he should he build three shelters for their guests. When the disciples look up it was only Jesus left standing there and he tells them to not be afraid. The next section is the healing of a demon possessed boy. Jesus' disciples were unable to cast out the demon because of their lack of faith. Jesus says that even faith as small as a mustard seed could move mountains. Jesus explains the importance of prayer and fasting, emphasizing the need for discipline when it comes to faith. In the last part of the chapter, Jesus instructs Peter to throw out his fishing line into the sea and tells him to take the coin out of the fishes mouth, showing God's power to provide.

In chapter 18, it teaches about the kingdom of heaven and having childlike humility is true greatness. True greatness in the kingdom is not about power and status, it is about humility. It says it is a major offense if anyone causes another person or child to stumble in their faith. If anyone causes another to stumble it would have been better if they drowned in the depths of the sea with an anchor around their neck. It gives a metaphor saying if a ligament causes them to sin to cut it off, and if the eyes cause them to sin, pluck it out. It is better to enter heaven with one eye than it is to enter hell with the full body and two eyes. There is a parable about a lost sheep which illustrates God's love and concern for each individual believer. For the son of man has come to save the lost. If only one sheep goes astray and the shepherd finds that single missing sheep, then the shepherd will rejoice more at the lost sheep that has been found over the ninety-nine who never went astray. After this, Jesus gives a lesson on addressing sin within the community, saying to correct them first, then reconcile and restore them within the church and community. It says Jesus will be in spirit there whenever people gather in his holy name. It ends with the parable of the unforgiving servant. Peter was asking what the limitations on forgiveness were and Jesus responds with this parable. There was a servant who was forgiven a large amount of debt, but when it was the other way around and only a small amount of debt was owed to him, the same servant choked out another the man to get his money back, refusing to forgive it. God expects the same forgiveness and mercy from his followers that God has shown them.

In chapter 19, Jesus traveled to the region of Judea to the other side of the Jordan and large crowds followed him. Some pharisees came to test him and ask if it is lawful for a man to divorce his wife for any reason. Jesus responds by quoting Genesis, where it says God created man and woman to come together as one flesh. The pharisees press him more asking what the point of divorce certificates were. Jesus explains that was a time where their hearts were hard, but unless someone commits sexual immorality, then it is not acceptable. The disciples say maybe it is better to never get married at all, Jesus understands that is not possible for everyone to remain single but if someone wants to do that, then that is acceptable too. Then people brought little children to Jesus asking to pray for them, the disciples try to send them away, but Jesus says the kingdom of heaven belongs to those who are innocent like these children. A rich young man approaches Jesus asking him what he must do to get eternal life, Jesus tells him to keep the commandments. The young man tells Jesus he has already kept all the commandments and asks what else he can do. Jesus replies to the young man telling him if he wants to be perfect, to sell all his possessions and wealth, donate it to the poor, and to come and follow the lord. When the young man heard this, he sadly walked away knowing he was not about to drop his whole life and donate all his possessions. This leads to Jesus telling his disciples it is harder for someone who is rich to enter the kingdom of heaven, and easier for a camel to go through the eye of a needle than it is for someone who is rich to enter the kingdom of God. This young man set up this perfect example because the attachment people have to this world, and their possessions is extremely hard to detach from. When the disciples heard this they were astonished and asked who is worthy of being saved. Jesus responds to them saying with God all things are possible, with man this is impossible. Peter says he dropped everything to follow Jesus, and asks what will there be for him and the others. Jesus replies saying that anyone who has given up their lives to follow him will receive a reward a hundred times as much and will inherit eternal life. Many who are first will be last, and many who are last will be first.

In chapter 20, there is a parable of workers in a vineyard. A landowner hires different workers at different hours and paid them all the same wage. Some have been working all day since morning, and others came in after five in the afternoon. The workers from the morning complain it is not fair they all got paid the same daily wage because they put in more work. The ones who worked all day agreed to that wage, they are just annoyed because the landowner was being extra generous to the half day workers. The landowner's generosity technically has nothing to do with the ones complaining because they agreed to that wage. The landowner says he has the right to do what he wants with his money, and tells them to take their pay and go. The point of the story is that God's kingdom is based on grace, not how much work they do or how long they have been a believer for. Then Jesus predicts his death a third time saying he will be handed over to be crucified, but will be raised to life on the third day. Jesus gets a request from a mother asking if he can save or grant seats at his right and left side. Jesus replies that she does not comprehend what she is asking. He explains that granting seats at the Father's side is not within his authority; those places are reserved for those for whom the Father has prepared them. Jesus said the son of man did not come to be served, but to serve, and to give his life as ransom for many. The chapter ends as Jesus and the disciples were leaving Jericho, a crowd was following them and when Jesus asked what they needed, they said they wanted their sight. Jesus had compassion on them and touched their eyes, immediately they received their sight and followed him. The last shall be first and the first last, many are called but few chosen.

In chapter 21, Jesus comes to Jerusalem as king. Israels leaders and Jesus follower's clash. Jesus pulls up on a donkey and the crowds roar for him, hailing him as the messiah with miraculous powers. Jesus comes in angry at the temple and goes right to the tax collectors and flips the table. Jesus asserts his authority and declares that his house will be called a house of prayer, but they are making it a den of thieves. Early the next day Jesus curses a fig tree because it cannot bear fruit, symbolizing God's judgement on those that fail to bear the fruit of faith and righteousness. At the temple, some chief priests came to Jesus and asked him on what authority he is doing these things. Jesus said he will answer their question if they answer his first. Jesus asks them if John the Baptist is from heaven or from human origin. They could not answer the question because the Jewish people consider John a prophet and it would turn the people against them if they say human origin, and if they answer heaven it will confirm Jesus' authority from God. The chapter ends with two parables. The two sons parable highlights the hypocrites who claim to obey God but do not, they are worse than those who refuse at first but come around, like the tax collectors and prostitutes. The parable of the wicked tenants portray God as the vineyard owner and the Jewish leaders as the tenants. They reject and kill the vineyard owners servants and even his own son, symbolizing their rejection of all God's messengers and Jesus himself.

In chapter 22, it starts with the parable of the wedding banquet where a king sends out invitations, but people refuse to come. This parable shows how the kingdom of God is open to everyone, not only Jews. The Pharisees and Herodians try to trap Jesus with a trick question about whether they should be required to pay taxes to Caesar. Jesus asks for a coin, points to Caesar's image on it and says, "give to Caesar what is Caesar's, and to God what is God's." They were amazed when they heard this, so they left him and went away. The Sadducees ask Jesus who a woman will be married to in the resurrection if she had multiple husbands. Jesus refutes this and says they will not be married in the resurrection and will be like angels in heaven. A lawyer asked Jesus which commandment is the greatest, Jesus quotes the old testament and says to love God with all the heart, soul, and mind and also to love your neighbor as yourself. Jesus highlights their limited understanding of what it means to be the messiah and what it means when he says he is both David's son and David's lord. He is revealing the messiah is not just a human descendant of David, but the divine son of God.

In chapter 23, it gives a warning against hypocrisy. The Jewish leaders did not practice what they preached, and Jesus says to follow the teachings of the scripture, not the examples of the Jewish leaders. These leaders are self-righteous always picking the nicest seats at the fancy places and always ask to be greeted with respect seeking glory for themselves. Jesus teaches humility and the great ones in God's kingdom live to serve others, not themselves. Jesus pronounces seven woes upon the scribes and pharisees for their hypocrisy and misleading teachings. He condemns them for blocking others from the kingdom of heaven, exploiting the vulnerable, appearing righteous while being corrupt, and persecuting God's prophets. The chapter ends with Jesus expressing sorrow for Jerusalem and those who reject Jesus and God's messengers. He foretells the city's destruction and that blessed are those who come in the name of the lord.

In chapter 24, it describes the destruction of the temple and signs of the end times where Jesus returns. There will be trials, tribulations, and deceptions to come. Believers are encouraged to stay strong, vigilant, and prepared for Christs return. Jesus predicts the destruction of the temple and warns about false prophets claiming to be God, many will come in his name claiming to be the messiah. There will be wars, rumors of wars, famines, earthquakes, persecution, and apostasy. It says the gospel of the kingdom will be preached in the whole world as a testimony to all nations, and then the end will come. Jesus references the prophet Daniel who spoke about these days calling it the abomination of desolation, signaling severe tribulation. Daniel was willing to die to not bow down to another God, and refused to renounce the lord. He accepted death over giving up his soul. His life is a testimony of bearing the cross for God. The return of Christ will be like lightning in the sky. Cosmic disturbances will signal the son of man's return. He will send angels with a trumpet call to gather his elect from all over the earth. When these times comes only God the Father will know when, nobody knows the day or hour, not even angels. Since no one knows when these prophecies will be fulfilled, it will come sudden and unexpected like Noah's flood. God urges believers to always be ready for his return because the end will come like a thief in the night.

In chapter 25, there is a parable of ten virgins used to symbolize the importance of being prepared for the second coming of Jesus Christ. It also has a parable of the bag of gold which symbolize using God given gifts and opportunities responsibly, not to neglect them. Then there is a parable of the sheep and goat, like when a shepherd separates sheep from goats. Jesus describes a final judgement where God will separate people into two groups, and the righteous will be celebrated for their kindness they have shown others who were hungry, thirsty, naked, and sick. The righteous will inherit eternal life while the wicked will be punished for their lack of compassion.

In chapter 26, Jesus' journey towards the cross begins. It illustrates his selflessness, love, and submission to the will of the Father. The chief priests and elders plot to arrest and kill Jesus, but not during the feast to avoid a riot. While Jesus was in Bethany in the home of Simon the leper, a woman poured an expensive jar of perfume on him. The disciples saw this and said how expensive that perfume was. Jesus said it was a beautiful thing she did for him, and she will be remembered for it when the gospel is preached to the world. Judas agrees to betray Jesus for thirty pieces of silver, and will give his location later when he has the opportunity. Jesus and his disciples celebrate the Passover. In this new practice, they will eat bread and drink wine in remembrance of him. During the meal at the last supper, Jesus foretells Judas betrayal and predicts Peter's denial. Peter says he would never betray and will die for him, but Jesus predicts that Peter will deny him three times before the rooster crows. Peter declared that even if he has to die with him, he will never disown him. Jesus takes his inner circle, Peter, James, and John into the garden of Gethsemane. He prays in deep agony, surrendering his will to the Father despite the coming suffering. Jesus gets seized and arrested, he asked if he is leading a rebellion based on how many weapons on hand his captors had. The disciples deserted the scene and fled. Jesus stands before the Sanhedrin and Peter followed him into the courtyard. Peters' denial comes as predicted, he faced heavy pressure from the crowd and was asked if he knew Jesus, he denied knowing him three times. He hears the crows and remembers Jesus' prediction just came true and starts weeping with tears because he loves Jesus and denied him.

In chapter 27, Judas was later filled with remorse and guilt; he ended up giving the silver back and killed himself. Jesus stands trial and is charged with blasphemy; Pilate from Rome did not see a criminal in front of him and saw no fault in Jesus, but fell to pressure from religious leaders and crowd. The chief priests and elders were manipulating and persuading the crowd to have Jesus executed. Pilate heard the crowd getting louder and said, "I am innocent of this man's blood; it is your responsibility." Jesus was sentenced to death by crucifixion. Jesus is mocked and beaten by the soldiers before being led to his death, where he is crucified alongside two robbers. They spit on him and take the staff and struck him on the head again and again. After three hours of darkness, Jesus gave up his spirit. At the moment of his death, the curtain of the temple was torn in two, the earth shook, and the rocks split. Joseph a follower of Jesus took the body, wrapped it in a clean linen cloth and placed it in his own new tomb that he had cut out of the rock. He rolled a big stone in front of the entrance of the tomb and went away. Mary Magdalene and the other Mary were sitting there observing where Jesus laid. The chief priests and pharisees secure Pilate's permission to seal and guard the tomb to prevent Jesus' disciples from stealing his body and claiming resurrection.

In chapter 28, Jesus has risen. Mary Magdalene and the other Mary discover the empty tomb and meet an angel who announces Jesus' resurrection. As they leave to inform the disciples, Jesus himself appears to them, confirming the resurrection and instructs them to tell the disciples to meet him in Galilee. The guards report the events to the chief priests, who conspire to spread a fake story that the disciples stole Jesus' body while the guards were sleeping. They bribe the soldiers to maintain this false account. Eleven disciples went to Galilee, to the mountain where Jesus had told them to go. The great commission is a final command from Jesus. He told the disciples that authority in heaven and on earth had been given to him. Therefore, for them to make disciples of all nations, baptizing them in the name of the Father and of the Son and of the Holy Spirit. Jesus said to teach the nations to obey everything he had commanded them, and God is with them always until the very end of the age.

Mark

The gospel of Mark is the oldest gospel. It was written by John Mark, who worked right next to Paul and a close partner with Peter. It was written in the first century, around the same time of Peter's death. He collected eyewitness testimonies of Jesus, and the book is broken up into sections of who Jesus is, the disciples, and how Jesus becomes the messiah. The gospel of Mark appears to be written for an audience in Rome. It has many recorded miracles and shows how people reacted to the good news of Jesus.

In chapter 1, Mark starts with first line saying, "The beginning of the good news about Jesus the Messiah, the Son of God." This was prophesied by the prophet Isaiah, who wrote that "A messiah King who is also a servant from the house of David will take our pain and bore our suffering, that he will be pierced for our transgressions and crushed for our iniquities, by his wounds we are healed." John the Baptist appears in the wilderness preaching repentance and baptism for the forgiveness of sins. The whole Judean countryside and all the people of Jerusalem went out to him confessing their sins. They were baptized by him in the Jordan River. At that time, Jesus came from Nazareth in Galilee and was baptized by John in the Jordan. As Jesus was coming up out of the water, he saw heaven being torn open and the spirit descending on him like a dove. A voice came from heaven, "You are my Son, whom I love; with you I am well pleased." Jesus is led into the wilderness by the spirit and is tempted by Satan for forty days. Jesus announces the good news of the kingdom of God, to repent and believe. He called on his first disciples with Simon and his brother Andrew, James, and John by the sea of Galilee. Jesus is casting out impure spirits and demons, the people were amazed and news spread about him quick. The sick people with various diseases came to him, Jesus healed many. A man with leprosy asked to be cleansed if the lord is willing, and Jesus said he is willing and for him to be clean, and he was cleansed.

In chapter 2, Jesus healed a paralyzed man and told him that his sins are forgiven. Forgiveness of sin is an authority that only God has, so people had some thoughts about that. The paralyzed man got up and walked away which amazed everyone and they praised God. Jesus was getting a lot of support from huge crowds, but there were still others who did not support him. Jesus calls Levi, a tax collector who is usually despised by society, but Jesus calls on all sinners from all parts of society. The disciples question Jesus about fasting, Jesus compares himself to bridegroom to signify that there will be a time more appropriate in the future after he is gone when they will fast. His teachings show that there will be a new covenant and new way of life after he is no longer with them. The priests and leaders rejected him and called his teachings blasphemy. There was controversy from the pharisees who challenged Jesus and his disciples for plucking grain on the sabbath. Jesus responds by saying he has authority over the law. He told them the sabbath was made for man, not man for the sabbath, so the son of man is lord of the sabbath. The pharisees plot to have him killed.

In chapter 3, Jesus heals a man's hand in the synagogue on the sabbath. After healing the man Jesus told him to stand up in front of everyone, and to stretch out his hand. Jesus asked which is lawful on the sabbath; to do good or to do evil, to save a life or to kill it. The Jewish leaders had no response and were angry, they plot to kill Jesus. Crowds followed him from Judea, Jerusalem, Idumea, and regions across the Jordan. Jesus appoints the twelve disciples. The disciples have the authority to drive out demons and are the appointed ones. Jesus gets accused by the teachers of law. They said things like he is out of his mind, and he had an impure spirit, which led Jesus to speak to them in parables saying whoever blasphemes against the holy spirit will be guilty of eternal sin. Then someone in the crowd told Jesus that his mother and brothers are looking for him, Jesus responds saying whoever follows God's will is his brother and sister and mother.

In chapter 4, when speaking to crowds Jesus used parables and metaphors, but when he was alone with his disciples, he explained everything. Jesus teaches the crowds about the kingdom of God. At the lake he teaches about the parable of the Sower, in this example God is the Sower and his word is the seed. The soils represent different types of people who hear the word, for example the path soil represent those who do not understand the word. Rocky ground represent those who receive the word with joy but go astray. Thorny ground represent the deceitfulness of wealth and how desires for things come in and choke the word. Good soil represent those who hear and accept the word, allowing it to take root and grow, resulting in a fruitful life. Jesus uses a lamp metaphor to emphasize that hidden truths will be revealed and the importance of hearing and spreading the word. A light is made to provide light, not to be hidden. Jesus shares a parable about a mustard seed. The seed grows mysteriously, and the tiny mustard seed becomes a large plant representing God's future kingdom that will expand and grow. The disciples cross the Sea of Galilee, and a violent storm arises. Jesus shows the scared disciples his authority and power over nature by rebuking the sea and the winds. He said quiet and be still, then the sea was completely calmed. He says to take courage and not be afraid.

In chapter 5, Jesus gives an exorcism to a demon-possessed man. The demons recognized Jesus' authority, and the demon begged to not be tortured. Jesus told the unclean spirit to come out of this man and to identify themselves. The demon says, "my name is Legion, for we are many." The demons begged Jesus to send their spirit to the large herd of pigs by the hillside. Jesus cast the demon out of the man into to pigs, then the herd of two-thousand pigs fell down a bank and drowned in a lake. Jesus raises a dead girl and heals a sick woman. He crossed over the lake by boat to the other side and a large crowd gathered around him. One of the synagogue leaders named Jairus pleaded to Jesus and said his little daughter is dying. Jesus took her by the hand and told her to get up, the girl stood up and began to walk around. There was a woman who had been bleeding for twelve years, and she kept suffering under the care of doctors; it only got worse, and she spent all she had. This women ran up behind Jesus and touched his cloak in desperation without asking first because she thought if she just touched his clothes, she will be healed. It worked and immediately she stopped bleeding, but Jesus felt that and asked the crowd who touched him. Jesus kept looking around to see who had done it and the women eventually told the truth and fell to her feet and told Jesus the whole truth while trembling with fear. Jesus looked at her and told her to go in peace and told her to be freed from her suffering.

In chapter 6, Jesus returns to his hometown and is met with skepticism and offense from his own people. Despite his miracles, they could not comprehend that the person they knew was the messiah. Jesus could not perform any miracles there, except lay his hands on a few sick people and heal them. He was amazed at their lack of faith. Jesus sends out the twelve disciples and gave them authority over impure spirits. His instructions for their journey were to bring nothing with them, only bring a staff, sandals, and the clothes on their backs. No bread, no bag, no money in their belts, not even an extra shirt. Jesus says do not be discouraged, if any place will not welcome them or listen to them, for them to shake it off their feet and use it as a testimony against them. The disciples went out and preached that people should repent, and they drove out many demons, anointed many sick people with oil, and healed them. John the Baptist was executed in jail by Herod on the request of Herodias daughter. She was encouraged to ask for that by her mother, and his head was served on a platter. Herodias held a grudge against John because he denounced her marriage, saying her marriage was unlawful. When Jesus landed, he sees a big crowd of people and his apostles gathered around him and reported to him all they had done and taught. Jesus took five loaves of bread and two fish, and multiplied them into baskets of food. The disciples distributed the food to five thousand people. After this, Jesus sends the disciples in boat across the sea, while he goes up on a mountainside to pray alone. During the night, the disciples see Jesus walking on water and were terrified because they thought it was a ghost. Jesus said to take courage and not be afraid, it is him. He calms their fears and gets in the boat which ended the wind. After they landing in Gennesaret, there were people from all over the region waiting and begging to be healed, and Jesus healed them.

In chapter 7, the pharisees and some of the teachers of the law who had come from Jerusalem gathered around Jesus and saw some of his disciple's eating food with hands that were not washed. The pharisees and teachers of the law asked Jesus, "Why don't your disciples live according to the tradition of the elders instead of eating their food with defiled hands?" Jesus replied and said, "Isaiah was right when he prophesied about you hypocrites; as it is written: these people honor me with their lips, but their hearts are far from me." Jesus explained that what defiles a person comes not from the outside, but from the heart. It is within a person's heart that evil thoughts arise such as sexual immorality, theft, murder, adultery, greed, malice, deceit, lewdness, envy, slander, arrogance and folly. All these evils come from inside and defile a person. Jesus left that place and went to the vicinity of Tyre. A Greek women came to Jesus and said her daughter was possessed by an impure spirit. She begged Jesus to drive the demon out of her daughter, and he cast the demon out of her. She went home and found her child lying on the bed, and the demon gone. After that, Jesus left the vicinity of Tyre and went through Sidon, he healed a deaf and a mute man. He told them not to tell anyone because people were overwhelmed with amazement and kept talking about it. Jesus told them not to tell anyone so it would not hinder his mission.

In chapter 8, another large crowd formed, and Jesus had compassion for these people because they have been with him three days and have not eaten. He takes seven loaves of bread and a few small fish, multiplies it and feeds a crowd of four thousand. He does more miracles like healing a blind man at Bethsaida. Jesus and his disciples went on to the villages around Caesarea Philippi. On the way Jesus asked them who do people say he is. They respond and say, some say John the Baptist, others say Elijah, and others say one of the prophets. Jesus asked what about him, and what does he think. Peter answered him and said, "You are the messiah." Jesus explains to his disciples what it means for him to be the messiah. He tells the disciples about his coming death and resurrection; his death is going to fix the hearts and bear sins of the world. The disciples are confused, do not fully understand the mission, and worried. Jesus predicts his death. He began to teach them that the son of man must suffer many things and be rejected by the elders, the chief priests, and the teachers of the law. He said that he must be killed and after three days rise again. Peter was not understanding it and tried to criticize Jesus. Jesus turned and looked at his disciples and tells Satan get behind him, and said that Satan does not have in mind the concerns of God, only human concerns. Jesus calls the crowd and the disciples to him. Jesus speaks and says whoever wants to be his disciple must deny themselves, and must be able to bear the cross to follow him. Whoever wants to save their life will lose it, but whoever loses their life for him and for the gospel will save it. What good is it for someone to gain the whole world, yet forfeit their soul? What can anyone give in exchange for their soul?

In chapter 9, after six days Jesus took Peter, James, and John with him and led them up a high mountain. Jesus turned white like a shining light, Elijah and Moses appeared and were talking with Jesus. Peter was so frightened and did not know what to say, he asks Jesus if he should make three shelters for all three of them. Then a cloud appeared and covered them. A voice came from the cloud saying, "This is my Son, whom I love. Listen to him." Suddenly, when they looked around, they no longer saw anyone with them except Jesus. Jesus reminds them to not to say anything or tell anyone what they saw until the son of man has been resurrected. The disciples were trying to figure out what rising from the dead even means. They are still confused as to what God's plan is. The disciples need to understand that this is a prophecy being fulfilled. Jesus refers to scripture and asks them why they think it is written about Elijah coming back and why the son of man must suffer and be rejected.

After this when they came to another crowd, Jesus heals a boy possessed by an impure spirit. The boy has been possessed since childhood and causes the boy to not be able to speak. Jesus drove it out and commanded the spirit to never come back to the body again. The disciples are unable to heal and drive out spirits, Jesus expresses his frustration by calling them the faithless generation. Jesus told them it can only be done through prayer, which shows the disciples level of faith is not ready yet. They left that place and passed through Galilee. Jesus did not want anyone to know where he was because he was teaching his disciples. Jesus predicts his death a second time and tells them that the son of man is going to be delivered into the hands of men. They will kill him, and after three days he will rise. They did not understand what he meant and were afraid to ask him about it. Jesus teaches them the nature of true greatness. He explains that to be first, one must be the very last, and the servant of all. Jesus warns about causing others to sin and the seriousness of sin. He encourages the disciples to be at peace with each other. Jesus tells them if their limbs or eyes cause them to sin, it is better to cut it off or pluck it out. It is better to enter heaven with one eye, rather than have two eyes and be thrown into hell, where the fire never goes out.

In chapter 10, Jesus leaves that place and went into the region of Judea and across the Jordan, crowds form around him again. The pharisees try to test Jesus by asking him if divorce is lawful. Jesus replies to the pharisees and asked them what Moses said. Jesus tells them their hard hearts are the reason Moses had to write them the law. In the beginning God created male and female, so they can join to become one flesh. What God has joined together, let no one separate. He says people should not get divorced unless someone commits adultery. Jesus blesses the little children and says that the kingdom of God belongs to those who receive it like a child. As Jesus was leaving, a man ran up to him and said he kept the commandments since he was a boy and asks Jesus what else he should do to inherit eternal life. Jesus tells the man to sell everything he has and give it to the poor, then he will have treasure in heaven. The man's face fell and walked away sad since he had wealth. It is harder for a rich man to enter the kingdom of heaven because they are less likely to give up their earthly possession, but all things are possible with God. They were on their way up to Jerusalem and Jesus predicts his death a third time. He took the twelve aside and told them what was going to happen to him. The son of man will be handed over to the officials, sentenced to death, and handed over to the gentiles. They will mock him, spit on him, beat him, and kill him. Three days later he will rise. James and John make a request to Jesus but do not understand the things they ask. They ask Jesus if one can sit to his left and the other to his right in his glory. Jesus told them they do not know what they are asking, and it is not for him to grant. Jesus says these places belong to those for whom they have been prepared. Greatness comes to those who serve and humble themselves. Even the son of man did not come to be served, but to serve, and to give his life as a ransom for many. Then they came to Jericho. Jesus and his disciples were together with a large crowd leaving the city, and a blind man named Bartimaeus heard that it was Jesus of Nazareth and started shouting for the son of David to have mercy on him. Many told him to be quiet, but the man just kept shouting. Jesus stepped in and told him to cheer up and stand. The man jumped to his feet and Jesus asked the guy what he can do for him. The man replies and said, rabbi I want to see. Jesus tells him go and his faith has healed him, and immediately the man received his sight.

In chapter 11, Jesus arrives in Jerusalem as king. Jesus sends two of his disciples to find a colt for his entry into Jerusalem. When he entered the city, crowds lay their cloaks and palm branches on the road, shouting "Hosanna! Blessed is the coming kingdom of our father David! Hosanna in the highest heaven!" He looked around at everything, but since it was already late, he went out to Bethany with the twelve. The next day Jesus curses a fig tree that had no figs, and he clears the temple courts. Jesus entered the temple courts and began driving out those who were buying and selling there. He overturned the tables of the money changers and the seats of those selling birds. Jesus declares the temple a house of prayer for all nations, not a den of robbers. He amazed the whole crowd. The chief priests and teachers of law start plotting how they are going to kill him. Jesus and his disciples head out of the city. The next morning, Peter points out a fig that Jesus cursed earlier for not having fruit. Jesus replies and says to have faith in God. Jesus says if anyone has no doubt in their heart and believes that what they say will happen, it will be done for them, and they can move mountains. Whatever they ask for in prayer, it will be theirs. Jesus says if anyone holds anything against anyone, forgive them so that their Father in heaven may forgive them for their trespasses. Jesus goes to Jerusalem and as he is walking in the temple courts, the chief priests, the teachers of the law, and the elders came to him and questioned his authority. They ask Jesus by what authority is he doing these things and who gave him authority. Jesus told them that he will tell them on what authority but for them to answer his question first. He asked, "was John's baptism from human origin or from heaven?" They discussed his question amongst themselves and realized whatever they answered was wrong because everyone held John as a legitimate prophet. One answer would turn the crowd against them and the other answer would confirm Jesus' authority from God. So, they could not answer the question and just said they do not know the answer. Jesus said okay then he is not answering their questions as to what authority he has.

In chapter 12, Jesus starts speaking to the crowd in parables. The parable of the wicked tenants is an extended analogy referring to God as a man who planted a vineyard, then rented out the vineyard to some farmers and moved to another place. When the man sends a servant to his vineyard to collect some fruit from the tenants, they seized him, beat him and sent him away empty-handed. Then he sent another servant, who was struck on the head and treated shamefully. Then he sent another, and that one they killed. He sent many others, some of them they beat, others they killed. He had one left to send, a son, whom he loved. He sent him last of all, saying, they will respect my son. Instead, the tenants use it as an opportunity for personal gain and say to one another, this is the heir let us kill him so the inheritance can be ours. So, they took him and killed him, then threw him out of the vineyard. Jesus asks, "what then should the owner of the vineyard do?" He will come and kill those tenants and give the vineyard to others. The vineyard is God's rule, and the tenants is the Jewish leadership, and the kingdom of God will be taken from them. The chief priests, the teachers of the law, and the elders realized that Jesus' parable is referencing them without even saying their names. They started to think of how they could arrest Jesus but were intimidated by the crowd, so they left him and went away.

Later on they sent some pharisees and Herodians to produce the perfect trick question to trap Jesus. The question is whether taxes should be paid to Caesar, either answer is wrong because it will either upset the romans who have guards present, or it will anger the Jewish crowd who pays an imperial tax. Jesus is aware of the trap and their hypocrisy; he asked to be brought a coin so he can look at it. They brought Jesus the coin and after inspecting it, he asks whose face is on the coin, they say it is Caesars face on the coin. Then Jesus says to them, give back to Caesar what is Caesar's and to God what is God's. The crowd was amazed, and the pharisees plan to catch him in his words was a failure. The Sadducees, who say there is no resurrection came to Jesus with a hypothetical question about afterlife, death, and marriage while referencing Moses law. Jesus corrects their understanding and explains that there will be no marriage in heaven. Jesus said when the dead rise, they will be like angels in heaven. He is not the God of the dead, but of the living. One of the teachers of the law came and heard them debating, he noticed Jesus gave them a good answer and asked him which commandment is the greatest of all the commandments. Jesus responds to the question and tells him to love the Lord your God with all your heart, all your soul, all your mind, and with all your strength. The second is to love your neighbor as yourself, there is no greater commandment than these. The teacher was impressed, and no one dared asking anymore questions. Jesus did some more teaching to the crowd in the temple courts and puzzles the crowd by questioning why the teachers say the messiah is the son of David. Jesus gives a warning to the teachers of law; they like to walk around in their fancy robes and be greeted with respect. They like to show off their status with the most important seats in the synagogues and the places of honor. They make lengthy prayers just for show, while exploiting the vulnerable and taking widows' houses. He says these men will be punished most severely. Jesus sat down where the offerings were put, he watched the crowd putting their money into the temple treasury. Many rich people gave a lot. A poor widow came by and put in just a few cents, which was everything she had left to her name. Jesus tells the disciples that this poor widow has put more into the treasury than all the others. She chose faith in God over the last few coins she needed for survival.

In chapter 13, as Jesus was leaving the temple, he makes a prophecy about the destruction of the temple and signs of the end times. One of his disciples points out how magnificent the buildings are and how massive the stones are. Jesus says that all of it will fall and not one stone will be left on another, every piece will be thrown down. On the Mount of Olives, Peter, James, John, and Andrew ask Jesus privately about the signs of these events. They ask when and what signs to look out for when they are about to be fulfilled. Jesus warns them about false prophets, wars, rumors of wars, and natural disasters as signs before the end. He said to watch out for deceivers because many will come in his name and claim to be him, many will be deceived. Nation will rise against nations and kingdoms against kingdoms, earthquakes, famines. It says not to worry because these things need to happen before the end. He refers to these things as birth pains before the end. Jesus foretells of the prosecution his followers will face in his name. They have to be willing to die for eternal life in the next. He said everyone will hate them because of him, but the one who stands firm until the end will be saved. Be on guard and ready because they will be handed over to authorities and persecuted. Because of Jesus, they will stand before governors and kings as witnesses to them. The gospel must be preached to all nations first. He says if they get arrested and about to go to trial, do not worry about what to say, just say whatever is given to them at the time by the holy spirit, which will do the speaking. Daniel prophesied the coming of the "abomination of desolation" which is a time of great tribulation. He warns about false prophets and deceivers who claim to be Christ. If anyone claims to be the messiah and performs miracles, do not believe it, even the elect will be fooled. It says to be on guard and to be alert because it will come like a thief in the night. He compares it to someone breaking into a house, and warns to not be asleep when that happens. After the tribulation or times of distress and anguish, cosmic signs from the sun, moon, and stars will appear. At that time Jesus will return, and people will see the son of man coming in clouds with great power and glory. He will send his angels to gather his elect from all corners of the earth. Jesus says to think of it like a fig tree, when you see the leaves fall out it means the next season is coming. When you see the signs, know that the end is near, right at the door. Jesus says no one knows the day or hour of the times, not even the angels in heaven. If he comes suddenly, do not let him find you sleeping. It is a warning for all people to watch out.

In chapter 14, the Passover and the festival of unleavened bread were only two days away. The chief priests and the teachers of the law were scheming to arrest Jesus secretly and kill him, but after the festival to prevent rioting. Jesus was in Bethany at Simon the leapers house and a women broke an expensive jar of perfume to pour it on Jesus' head to prepare for his burial. Some of the people present criticized her for waste, saying the perfume is like a year's wage which could have been sold and used to give to the poor. Jesus rebuked them and said to not bother her, because what she did for him was a beautiful thing and will be remembered when the gospel spreads to the entire world. On the first day of the festival of unleavened bread, Jesus and his disciples have the last supper. On this day it is customary to sacrifice a Passover lamb, so the disciples ask where he wants them to go and prepare for him to eat. Jesus sends two disciples to go to the city. He tells them a man carrying a glass jar of water will meet them, and for them to follow the man into a house. Jesus said he will show them a large furnished room upstairs that is ready for preparations. The disciples left to the city; found the things Jesus told them and prepared the Passover. When evening came, Jesus arrived with the twelve. While they were at the table eating, Jesus announces that one of them will betray him, someone who is eating at the table right now. They were saddened, and one by one they were saying it is not them. Jesus replies and says it is one of the twelve and woe to the man who betrays the son of man, it would be better for him if he had not been born. While they were eating Jesus identified the bread as his body and the wine as his blood of the new covenant. He will not drink again from the fruit of the vine until he drinks it in God's new kingdom.

They sang a hymn and then went to the Mount of Olives. Jesus predicts Peter's denial before the rooster crows twice. Peter gets emotional and insists empathetically he would never do this; he cannot believe it because he loves Jesus too much. Peter says even if he must die with him, he will never disown him. The others agree and they are ready for the mission. They went to a place called Gethsemane and Jesus took Peter, James and John along with him. Jesus looked deeply troubled and distressed; he said his soul was overwhelmed with so much sorrow to the point of death. Jesus asked them to stay and keep watch while he prays. Jesus went a little further out, fell to the ground and prayed that if possible the hour might pass from him, he will follow God the Fathers will. Jesus returns to the disciples and finds them sleeping. He tells them to keep watch and pray so they do not fall into temptation, because the spirit is willing, but the flesh is weak. Once more he went away and prayed for the same thing. When Jesus came back, he found them sleeping again because their eyes were heavy. Jesus tells them to rise and get up because the hour has come for the son of man to be delivered into the hands of the sinners. Just as Jesus was speaking, Judas his disciple appeared with a crowd armed with swords and clubs, who were sent from the chief priests, the teachers of the law, and the elders. The betrayer Judas made up a signal to point out Jesus for the arrest. The signal was a kiss, and he walked up to Jesus and greeted him with a kiss. The men seized Jesus and arrested him. One of Jesus disciples drew the sword from one of the high priests' servants and cut off his ear. Jesus asked his captors if he is leading a rebellion or something because of how aggressively they come at him with swords and clubs to capture him. Jesus said everyday he was teaching in the temples and was not arrested; this means the prophecy is being fulfilled. Then everyone deserted Jesus and fled.

They took Jesus to the Sanhedrin, which is a council of Jews. The high priest, all the chief priests, the elders, and the teachers of the law came together. They were looking for evidence against Jesus so they could put him to death but could not find any. Someone stood up and gave false testimony against him saying, "Jesus said he will destroy the temple." It was nonsense, and their testimonies did not even agree. Jesus remained silent and did not answer. The high priest asked him if he is the messiah, the son of the blessed one. Jesus said yes, he is the messiah, and they will see the son of man sitting at the right of the mighty one coming from the clouds of heaven. The high priest tore his clothes and said they do not need any more witnesses because everyone heard the blasphemy themselves and all of them condemned him as worthy of death. Then some began to spit at Jesus, blindfolded him, and struck him with their fists. The guards took him and beat him. Peter was below in the courtyard and one of the servant girls of the high priest came by. She recognized Peter as being with Jesus and called him out. Peter said he does not know what she is talking about and walked away into the entryway. The servant girl saw Peter in the entryway and called him out again, she pointed him out and said this fellow is one of them. Again, Peter denied it. After a little while of sitting there, the people close by told Peter he is a Galilean, and he must be one of them. Peter swore that he did not know the man they are talking about. Immediately the rooster crowed the second time. Then Peter remembered the words Jesus had spoken to him about denying him, he broke down and wept realizing what he had done.

In chapter 15, Jesus stands before Pontius Pilate, the governor of Judea. Early in the morning, the chief priests, teachers of law, and elders bound Jesus and handed him over to Pilate. Pilate asked Jesus twice if he was king of the Jews and if he was going to answer to all these accusations. Jesus said, " you have said so" and did not reply to the accusations. It was custom at the festival to release a prisoner the crowd requested. There was a man called Barabbas who is charged for murder, and Pilate asks the crowd if they want Barabbas or the king of the Jews to be released. The chiefs priest stirred up and manipulated the crowd to release Barabbas instead of Jesus. Pilate asks the crowd what he should do with the one they call king of the Jews, and they shouted to crucify him. Pilate wanted to please the crowd, so he had Jesus flogged and handed over to be crucified. The soldiers led Jesus away into the palace, put a purple robe on him, then twisted together a crown of thorns to set it on him. They mocked Jesus saying hail the king of the Jews as he is bleeding with the crown. They repeatedly struck him on the head with a staff and spit on him. After mocking him, they led him out to crucify him. Simon of Cyrene carried the cross and they brought Jesus to the place called Golgotha, which means place of the skull. They crucified him and divided up his clothes. It was nine in the morning when they crucified him.

The written charge against him read, "King of the Jews." They crucified two criminal thieves with Jesus, one to his left and the other to his right. This is the prophecy in Isaiah where it says Jesus will be numbered with the transgressors. The bystanders were shouting insults at him and shaking their head. They challenged Jesus to come down and save himself. The chief priests and teachers were making jokes saying he can save others but cannot save himself.

At noon, darkness came over the whole land until three in the afternoon. At three in the afternoon Jesus yells out, "God why have you forsaken me." Jesus was offered a drink on a stick, someone intervenes and says leave him and let us see if Elijah comes to take him down. The temple of the curtain was torn from top to bottom when Jesus gave his last breath. A centurion, witnessing these events, acknowledges Jesus as the Son of God. Mary Magdalene, Mary the mother of James the younger and of Joseph, and Salome were watching from a distance. In Galilee, some of these women had followed him and cared for his needs. It was a day before the sabbath and as the evening approached, Joseph of Arimathea went to Pilate and asked for Jesus' body. Pilate was surprised to hear that Jesus was already dead, he confirmed with his roman officer that it was indeed true. Pilate agreed to give him the body. Joseph bought some linen cloth, took down the body, wrapped it in the linen, and placed it in a tomb cut out of rock. Then he rolled a stone against the entrance of the tomb. Mary Magdalene and Mary the mother of Joseph, saw where he was laid.

In chapter 16, when the Sabbath was over, Mary Magdalene, Mary the mother of James, and Salome bought spices so they can go anoint Jesus' body. Early on the first day of the week after sunrise they went to the tomb. Just as they were asking each other who is going to roll the stone away from the entrance, they looked up and saw that the stone had already been moved. They enter they tomb, and an angel is there that informs them that Jesus has risen and instructs them to tell the disciples and Peter. They were overcome with awe and fear, they initially fled and said nothing because they were afraid.

Added context- The ending of Mark from verse nine through twenty have been noted on most Bibles and debated if they really existed. Codex Sinaiticus does not contain this ending of Mark. The end of a gospel is the most vulnerable part, and many scholars do not believe it is inspired word.   This is the ending after verse nine in the last chapter. Jesus appears first to Mary Magdalene, who then tells the disciples. They refuse to believe her. Jesus appears to two disciples; nobody believed them either. Later Jesus appeared to the eleven as they were eating, he criticized them for their lack of faith and their stubborn refusal to believe those who had seen him after he had risen. Jesus told them to go into all the world and preach the gospel to all creation. Whoever believes and is baptized will be saved, signs will accompany those who believe. In his name they will drive out demons and speak in tongues, they will place their hand on sick people, and they will get well. After the Lord Jesus had spoken to them, he was taken up into heaven and he sat at the right hand of God. Then the disciples went out and preached everywhere, and the lord worked with them and confirmed his word by the signs that accompanied it.

Luke

Luke addresses Theophilus, stating his aim to write an orderly account of the events that have been fulfilled among them. These are the passages in Luke that are not in the other gospels.

1:5-25 The Promise of the Birth of John the Baptist- Zechariah, a priest, is visited by the angel Gabriel while serving in the temple. Despite Zechariah and his wife Elizabeth's old age, Gabriel foretells the birth of a son, John, who will prepare the way for the Lord. Zechariah doubts the angel's words and is struck mute until the prophecy's fulfillment.

1:26-38 The Proclamation- God sent the angel Gabriel to visit the virgin Mary from Nazareth and tells her she will conceive a son. Mary is pledged to Joseph, a descendant of David. The son's name is Jesus, who will reign over Jacob's house forever and his kingdom will never end. Mary wonders how this is possible because she is a virgin. Gabriel assures her this will be through the holy spirit and the power of the most high will overshadow her. Even Elizabeth, Mary's relative who is old in age will conceive a child. Mary sees Elizabeth's miraculous pregnancy as a sign and submits to God's will.

1:39-45 Mary's Visit to Elizabeth- Mary hurried to a town in the hill country of Judea and entered Zechariah's home and greeted Elizabeth. When Elizabeth heard Mary's greeting, the baby leaped into her womb and Elizabeth was filled with the holy spirit. Elizabeth blesses Mary for believing and confirms Mary will conceive a child.

1:45 -56 Mary's song- Mary sings a song of praise, glorifying God and his mercy, and his promise to Israel since Abrahams descendants. God has brought down rulers from their thrones and lifted up the humble.

1:57-66 The Birth of John the Baptist- Elizabeth gives birth to a son and on the eighth day when they came to circumcision the baby, Zechariah confirms his son's name as John, regaining his speech and praising God. Her neighbors and relatives heard that the lord had shown her great mercy, and they shared her joy. The baby spoke praising God, and the neighbors were in awe and shock, then word spread quickly around the hill country of Judea. The people of Judea recognized that the baby was divine, and the lord's hand was with him.

1:66-80 Zechariah- Filled with the holy spirit, Zechariah prophesies about the roles his son John will play in God's salvation plan through the line of David. Zechariah sees God's plan for the child is to prepare a way for the lord, to give his people the knowledge of salvation through the forgiveness of their sins. The Lord God showed their ancestors mercy and kept his covenant, the oath sworn to the father Abraham. John is growing strong in spirit and living in the wilderness until his public appearance to Israel.

2:21-40 Presentation in the Temple- Mary and Joseph present Jesus at the temple according to the laws of Moses. There was a man in Jerusalem called Simeon, who was righteous and devout. The holy spirit came upon Simeon, and it was revealed to him about the messiah. Moved by the spirit, he went into the temple. When the parents brought in the child Jesus to do for him what the custom of the law required, Simeon took the baby in his arms and praised God. Simeon started praying with the baby in his hand saying that the sovereign lord promised, and he may dismiss his servant in peace, and he has seen God's salvation. The child's father and mother marveled at what was said about him. Simeon blessed them and told Mary about the future of the child. A prophet named Anna also gives thanks, she speaks about Jesus to all awaiting redemption. After Joseph and Mary did everything required by law, they returned to Galilee to their own town of Nazareth. The child grew and became strong; he was filled with wisdom, and the grace of God was on him.

2:41-52 Young Jesus in the Temple- Every year Jesus' parents went to Jerusalem for the Festival of the Passover. When Jesus was there at twelve years old, the festival that year was over and his parents were returning home when they realized Jesus stayed behind in Jerusalem without the parents noticing. They traveled for a day before realizing he was not there and began looking for him among relatives and friends. When they did not find him, they went to Jerusalem to find him. After three days they found him in the temple courts, sitting among the teachers, listening to them and asking them questions. Everyone who heard him was amazed at his understanding and his answers. When his parents found him, they were astonished, they told him they were anxiously searching for him and how he could treat them like that. The boy told them he thought they would know he had to be at his Father's house referring to God, but they did not understand what he was talking about. He went down to Nazareth with them and was obedient to them. His mother treasured all these things in her heart. Jesus grew in wisdom and stature, and in favor with God and man.

3:7-14 John's Preaching- It is John the Baptist preparing the way. John spoke to the crowd that came to be baptized, asking them who warned them to flee from the coming wrath. John says to produce fruit in keeping with repentance and every tree that does not produce good fruit will be cut down and thrown into the fire. When the people asked him what they should do, he tells them if a man has two shirts and the other has zero, to share with the one who does not, same concept for helping people who do not have food. When the soldiers ask John what they should do, he tells them to not extort money, do not accuse people falsely, and to be content with what they have. People started to wonder in their hearts whether John was the messiah. John tells them that someone who is more powerful than him will come, one whose sandals straps he is not worthy to untie. John tells them this man will baptize them with the holy spirit and fire.

3:23-38- A genealogy tracing Jesus' parents tracing back to David.

5:1-11 The Miraculous Catch of Fish- One day when Jesus was standing by the lake of Gennesaret, the people were crowding around him and listening to the word of God. He saw two boats at the water's edge, left there by the fishermen, who were washing their nets. He got into one of the boats, the one belonging to Simon, and asked him to put it out a little from shore. Then he sat down and instructed the people from the boat. Jesus told Simon to put the net into the deep water and let the nets down for a catch. Simon tells Jesus they have been out there all night and have not caught anything, but he will try what Jesus said and let down the nets. When they had done so, they caught such a large number of fish that their nets began to break. They signaled their partners in the other boat to come and help them, and they came and filled both boats so full that they began to sink. He and all his companions were astonished at the catch of fish they had taken, Simon fell at Jesus knees and said to stay away from him because he is a sinful man. James and John, who were Simon's partners, were also amazed. Then Jesus told Simon to not be afraid, from now on they will fish for people. So they pulled their boats up on shore, left everything and followed him.

6:20-26 Blessings and Woes- Jesus looks at his disciples and says blessings. Blessed are the poor, for theirs is the kingdom of God. Blessed are the hungry ones, they will be satisfied, and blessed are the ones who weep, they will laugh. Blessed are those when people hate them, when they exclude them, insult them, and reject their name as evil, because of the son of man. Rejoice in that day and leap for joy because there is great reward in heaven. This is how prophets were treated by ancestors in the past. A woe serves as a warning, a call to repentance, and a reminder of the need for forgiveness through faith in Jesus Christ. Woe to those who are rich because they have already received their comfort. Woe to those who are well fed now, they will go hungry. Woe to those who laugh now, for they will mourn and weep. Woe to those who everyone speaks well of, for that is how their ancestors treated the false prophets.

7:11-17 The Widow's Son at Nain- Jesus raises a widows son from the dead. Jesus went to a town called Nain with his disciples and a large crowd went along with him. As he approached the town gate, a dead person was being carried out, the only son of a widow. The lord saw her and his heart went out to her; he told her not to cry. Jesus went up and touched the stand they were carrying the dead son on and said, "young man I say to you to get up." The dead man sat up and began to talk, and Jesus gave him back to his mother. The crowd were all filled with awe and praised God. They said a prophet has appeared before them and God has come to help his people. This news about Jesus spread throughout Judea and the surrounding country.

8:1-3 Mary Magdalene- Jesus traveled from one town and village to the next, proclaiming the good news of the kingdom of God. The twelve were with him and Mary Magdalene, who had been cured of evil spirits and diseases, seven demons had come out.

9:52-56 Jesus is Rejected by Samaritans- As the time approached for him to be taken up to heaven, Jesus resolutely set out for Jerusalem. He sent messengers who went into a Samaritan village to get things ready for him, but he was not welcomed because he was heading for Jerusalem. When disciples James and John saw this they asked Jesus if they should punish and destroy them, Jesus rebuked them, and they went to another village instead.

10:17-20 The Return of the Seventy- The seventy-two returned with joy telling Jesus that the demons submit to them in his name. Jesus tells them he has seen Satan fall like lightning from heaven. The lord has given them authority to trample snakes and scorpions and to overcome all the power of the enemy; nothing will harm them. However, Jesus tells them to not rejoice that the spirits submit to them but rejoice that their names are written in heaven.

10:29-37 The Parable of the Good Samaritan- In the parable of the good Samaritan, the expert in law and Jesus discussed loving God and a neighbor as yourself. The teacher wanted a further explanation and asked who his neighbor is. Jesus tells a parable about a man who was attacked by robbers when he was going down from Jerusalem to Jericho. They stripped him of his clothes, beat him, and left him half dead. A priest and a Levite happened to be going down the same road and after seeing the man, they went to the other side of the road. But a traveling Samaritan came where the man was and when he saw him, he took pity on him. He went to him and bandaged his wounds, pouring on oil and wine. Then he put the man on his own donkey, brought him to an inn and took care of him. The next day he gave payment to the innkeeper and told them to look after him, and if any additional expenses come up, he will reimburse them when he returns. Jesus asks which of those three men was a neighbor to the man who was beaten by the robbers, the expert of law says the one who had mercy on him. Jesus says to do likewise.

10:38-42 Mary and Martha- As Jesus and his disciples were on their way, he came to a village where a woman named Martha opened her home to him. She had a sister called Mary, who sat at the lord's feet listening to what he said. Martha was distracted with all the preparations and asked the lord if her sister should help her and not leave her with all the work. Jesus responds by saying Martha's name twice and telling her she is worried and upset about the many things. He tells Martha that only few things are needed or indeed only one. Jesus says Mary's choice to listen to his teachings is better, and it will not be taken away from her.

11:5-8 A Friend at Midnight- After teaching the lord's prayer, Jesus tells this parable. Suppose someone has a friend; they knock on their friends door at midnight and ask for three loaves of bread. Suppose the one inside answers and says do not bother him. The doors are already locked, and he and his children are already in bed. He says he cannot get up and give him anything. Even though he will not get up and give him the bread because of friendship, because of his shameless audacity he will surely get up and give him as much as he needs. Jesus says to ask, and it will be given, seek and it will be found, knock and the door will be opened. Everyone who asks receives, the one who seeks finds, and to the one who knocks, the door will be opened.

11:27-28 True Blessedness- A woman in the crowd called out to Jesus and said blessed is the mother who gave you birth and nursed you. Jesus replied to the women and said blessed rather are those who hear the word of God and obey it.

12:13-21 Warning against Greed and The Parable of the Rich Fool- Someone in the crowd spoke to Jesus and said teacher, tell my brother to divide the inheritance with him. Jesus responds by asking who appointed him a judge to settle this dispute. Jesus said for them to watch out and be on guard against all kinds of greed, because life is not about an abundance of possessions. Jesus tells them a parable of a rich man who yielded an abundant harvest. The man thought to himself, wondering what he should do with all the extra crops because there is not enough space to store them. Then the man decided he will tear down his barn and build a bigger one to put the surplus of crops. He will have plenty of grain saved up for years and will take life easy. That very night he dies, and God calls him a fool because now who is going to get what he prepared for himself. This is how it will be with whoever stores things up for themselves but is not rich toward God.

13:1-5 Repentance or Destruction- This is a call to repentance. In response to questions about the Galileans whose blood Pilate had mixed with sacrifices, and those killed by a falling tower. Jesus emphasizes the need for personal repentance to avoid perishing.

13:6-9 The Parable of the Barren Fig Tree- Jesus tells a parable about a fruitless fig tree that shows God's patience and the urgent need for repentance. A man had a fig tree growing in his vineyard, but the tree did not produce any fruit. He told the vineyard caretaker to cut it down because it is a waste of soil. The vineyard caretaker asked for one more year to fertilize it and if it does not have fruit next year, then cut it down. The meaning of the parable is to explain that God is the vineyard owner and expects fruits from individuals.

13:10-17 The Healing of the Crippled Woman on the Sabbath- On a sabbath, Jesus was teaching in one of the synagogues, and there was a woman there who had been crippled by a spirit for eighteen years. She could not straighten up at all. When Jesus saw her, he called her forward and set her free from her disability. As soon as Jesus put his hands on her, she immediately straightened up and praised God. The outraged synagogue leader told the people that there are six days for work, so if they want to be healed to come on those days, not the sabbath. The lord called them hypocrites because they are guilty themselves of doing things on the sabbath, like working on the animals. Jesus said should not this woman, who is a daughter of Abraham, whom Satan has kept bound for eighteen long years, be set free on the sabbath from what bound her. When Jesus said this, all his opponents were humiliated, but the people were delighted with all the wonderful things he was doing.

13:31-33 Herod- The pharisees came to Jesus and said "leave this place and go somewhere else. Herod wants to kill you."

14:1-6 The Healing of the Man- One sabbath, Jesus was eating in the house of a prominent pharisee, he was being carefully watched. In front of Jesus was a man suffering from abnormal swelling of his body. Jesus asked the pharisees if it was lawful to heal on the sabbath or not. They remained silent, so Jesus took hold of the man, healed him and sent him on his way. Then Jesus proceeded to ask them if it were their child or animal who fell on sabbath day, would they not immediately pull them out. They had nothing to say.

14:7-14 Teaching on Humility- Jesus notices that guests pick places of honor at the tables. Jesus says to take the lowest position or seat instead. He encourages the host to invite those who cannot repay, the poor and disabled, promising blessings for such generosity. Those who humble themselves will be exalted. They will be repaid at the resurrection of the righteous

15:8-10 The Parable of the Lost Coin- Jesus says suppose a woman had ten coins and loses one, she uses a light and searches the house carefully until she finds it. When she finds it, she tells her friends and neighbors how happy she is to find her coin. Jesus says this is what it is like for him to have just one repented sinner saved.

15:11-32 The Prodigal Son- This is also known as the parable of the lost son, which follows the parables of the lost sheep and the lost coin. Jesus demonstrated what it means to be lost, how heaven celebrates with joy when the lost are found, and how the loving Father longs to save people. Jesus tells of a man who has two sons, the younger son wants his inheritance, so the father gives it to him. Soon after that, the younger son gathered everything he had and set off to a distant country. While in the other country, he squandered his wealth with reckless spending and wild living. Then the country he set off to faced severe famine, and he became needy. He got hired by a citizen of that country and was sent out to feed the pigs. While watching the pigs eat, he longed to have a full stomach, but no one gave him anything. He came to his senses and realized his father's servants are eating better than he is, while he is out here starving to death. He decides that he will set out to go back to his father and tell him he made a huge mistake; he will tell his father he has sinned against heaven and his father. That he is no longer worthy to be his son, and to hire him as one of his servants. So, he came home and went to his father who saw his youngest son from a distance. The father ran to his son filled with compassion and threw his arms around him and kissed him. He tells his father he has sinned against heaven and him, and that he is no longer worthy to be called his son. The father immediately calls one of his servants to bring the best robe, ring, and sandals to put on his son. Then to bring the fattest calf to kill so they can feast and celebrate. The father thought his son was dead and was simply happy that he was alive, he was lost but now found, so they began to celebrate. Meanwhile, the oldest son came from the field to the house because he heard music and dancing. The older son asked the servant what was going on, and the servant tells him that his brother has come back, and that his father killed the fattest calf because his son is home unharmed. The older brother became angry and refused to go in, so his father went out and pleaded with him. He said to his father, for all these years he has been working hard slaving himself away for him, he never disobeyed but never received anything. He said he did not even get a young goat so he could celebrate with his friends. He tells his father that his brother squandered his property and money chasing pleasure, and now he does not understand why the younger brother is getting rewarded with the fattest calf. The father responds by saying that he has always been with him, and that everything he has is also his. The father says they need to celebrate because he thought his brother was dead and is just happy to see him alive, he was lost but now found. This shows how God views humans, it teaches the importance of God's unconditional love, and the power of transformative repentance.

16:1-15 The Parable of the Shrewd Manager- Jesus shares a parable about a dishonest manager who, when faced with the loss of his job, tried to be clever or cunning to secure his own future by reducing the debts owed to his boss by others. Jesus says whoever can be trusted with very little can also be trusted with a lot, and whoever is dishonest with very little will also be dishonest with a lot. If someone is not trustworthy with someone else's property, who will give them property of their own. If someone has not been trustworthy in handling worldly wealth, who is going to trust them with true riches. No one can serve two masters; they cannot serve both God and money. The pharisees, who loved money, heard all this and were sneering at Jesus. He told the pharisees they are the ones who justify themselves in the eyes of others, but God knows their hearts. What people value highly is detestable in God's sight.

16:19-31 The Rich Man and Lazarus -There was a rich man, he dressed in purple and fine linen, living in luxury every day. There was a beggar at his gate named Lazarus, covered with sores. Lazarus would eat what fell from the rich man's table, the dogs would even come and lick his sores. A time came when the beggar died, and the angels carried him to Abrahams side. The rich man also died and was buried. The rich man was in torment in hades, he looked up and saw Abraham far away with Lazarus by his side. So, the man asked Father Abraham to have pity on him, and if Lazarus can dip the tip of his finger in water and cool his tongue, because he is in agony in the fire. Abraham replied to the rich man by saying "Son, remember that in your lifetime you received your good things, while Lazarus received bad things, now he is comforted here, and you are in agony. Regardless, between them is a barrier of great separation that's set-in place, those that want to go from here to there cannot, nor can anyone cross over from there to us." The man begged to send Lazarus to his family and his five brothers to warn them, so they do not have to go to this place of torment. Abraham told him that God already sent Moses and the prophets; they can listen to them. The man pleaded by saying if someone who is already dead goes to them, there is a better chance his family can repent. Abraham tells him if they will not listen to Moses and the prophets, then they will not be convinced even if someone rises from the dead.

17:7-10 We are Servants -Jesus teaches about the importance of service. He tells a parable about a servant who is thanked for their service, but it should not be expected. It shows that fulfilling God's duties is simply doing what is expected.

17:11-19 Jesus Heals Ten Men with Leprosy- On his way to Jerusalem, Jesus traveled along the border between Samaria and Galilee. As he was going into a village, ten men who had leprosy met him. They stood at a distance and said, "Jesus, Master, have pity on us," When Jesus saw them, he told them go and show themselves to the priests. As they went to do that, they were cleansed. When one of them realized he was healed, he came back and started praising God in a loud voice. He threw himself at Jesus' feet and thanked him. Jesus asked, "I thought all ten were cleansed, where are the other nine? Has no one returned to give praise to God except this foreigner?" Then Jesus tells him to rise and to go, his faith made him well.

17:20-21 The Kingdom of God- The pharisees ask Jesus when the kingdom of God would come and Jesus tells them the coming of the kingdom of God is not something that can be observed, nor will people say it is here or there. It is because the kingdom of God is in the midst.

18: 1-8 The Parable of the Persistent Widow- The persistent widow is a parable that Jesus told in order to teach his disciples about the importance or prayer and perseverance. It involves a widow who repeatedly asks an unjust judge for justice against her adversary. Even though the judge initially refuses to help her, eventually he grants her request because of her persistence. God will bring justice for his chosen ones who are persistent in faith and call out to him day and night, he will not put them off.

18:9-14 The Parable of the Pharisee and the Tax Collector- Jesus tells a parable for those who are confident in their own righteousness and look down on everyone else. Two men go to the temple to pray, one pharisee and one tax collector. The pharisee stood by himself and prayed, he thanked God that he is not like these other people, like robbers, evildoers, adulterers, or even like this tax collector. The pharisee tells God he fasts twice a week and gives a tenth of what he has. On the other hand, the tax collector ashamed to even look up to heaven, prayed to God admitting he is a sinner and to have mercy on him. The tax collector went home justified before God. For all those who exalt themselves will be humbled, and those who humble themselves will be exalted.

19:41-44 Jesus Weeps over Jerusalem- This was after he entered Jerusalem as king. As Jesus approached Jerusalem and saw the city, he wept over it and says if they only knew this day would bring them peace, but it is hidden from their eyes. The days will come when Israel's enemies will build an embankment that holds back water into the city, encircling them and trap them in from every side. They will demolish them and their children to the ground within their walls. They will not leave one stone on another, because they did not recognize the time God came to them.

21:34-36 Day of the Lord- Jesus says to be careful in these days, hearts will be weighed down with carousing, drunkenness, and the anxieties of life. The day of judgement will close in suddenly like a trap, it will come on all those who live on the face of the earth. Always be on the watch and pray that you might be able to escape all that is about to happen, and stand before the son of man.

21:37- 38 Ministry of Jesus- Each day Jesus was teaching at the temple, and each evening he went out to spend the night on the hill called the Mount of Olives. All the people came early in the morning to hear him at the temple.

22:35-38 End of Last Supper- Jesus asked his disciples if they lacked anything when he sent them out without a purse, bag, or sandals and they replied saying no. He tells them to trade their cloaks for a sword if they do not have one. They were numbered with the transgressors, and this must be fulfilled in him. What is written about him is reaching its fulfillment. The disciples say, "see lord here are the two swords," and then Jesus says that is enough.

Further explained- Jesus commanding them to buy swords symbolizes the spiritual warfare and challenges that his disciples would encounter in the future. The swords represent the disciples' need to arm themselves with spiritual strength and perseverance. They need steadfast faith to confront the trials and opposition they would face in spreading the message of the gospel. The call to buy swords in this context symbolizes the disciples' readiness to face persecution and spiritual battles as they embark on their mission to spread the teachings of Jesus.

23:6-12 During the Hearing of Jesus- The chief priests and crowd accuse Jesus in front of Pilate saying he stirred people up all over Judea starting in Galilee. Pilate asked if the man was a Galilean. When he learned that Jesus was under Herod's jurisdiction, Jesus was sent to Herod who was also in Jerusalem at the time. When Herod saw Jesus, he was greatly pleased because for a long time he had been wanting to see him. From what he had heard about him, he hoped to see him perform a sign of some sort. He asked him many questions, but Jesus gave no answer. The chief priests and the teachers of the law were standing there, vehemently and forcefully accusing him. Then Herod and his soldiers ridiculed and mocked him. They dressed him in an elegant robe, and sent him back to Pilate. That day Herod and Pilate became friends, before this they had been enemies.

23:13-16 Pilate says Jesus' innocence- Pilate called together the chief priests, the rulers, and the people. Pilate tells them they brought him this man, who is said to be inciting the people to rebellion, but after examining him in their presence, he has found no basis for the charges against him. He said that neither has Herod who sent him back, and that Jesus has done nothing to deserve death. Pilate says he will punish him, then release him.

24:36-43 Jesus Appears to the Disciples- While the disciples were talking, Jesus himself appears among them and tells them peace be with them. They were startled and frightened, thinking they saw a ghost. Jesus asks them why they are troubled and why doubts arise in their minds. Jesus tells them to look at his hands and feet, for them to touch him because a ghost does not have flesh or bones, which he had. They were in joy and amazement. Then Jesus asks if they have anything to here to eat, they gave him a piece of broiled fish. Jesus took the fish and ate it in their presence.

John

1:1 The Word became Flesh- In the beginning was the Word, and the Word was with God, and the Word was God. He was with God in the beginning. Through him all things were made; without him nothing was made that has been made. In him was life, and that life was the light of all mankind. The light shines in the darkness, and the darkness has not overcome it. There was a man sent from God whose name was John. He came as a witness to testify concerning that light, so that through him all might believe. He himself was not the light; he came only as a witness to the light.

1:35-51 The Call of the First Disciples- John the Baptist points out Jesus to his disciples, two of whom follow Jesus. Andrew, one of them, brings his brother Simon (Peter) to Jesus. Jesus also calls Philip, who brings Nathanael. Jesus impresses Nathanael by displaying his supernatural knowledge.

2:1-12 The Miracle at Cana Wedding- Jesus, his mother, and his disciples attend a wedding in Cana. When the wine runs out, Jesus miraculously turns water into wine. What Jesus did here in Cana of Galilee was the first of the signs through which he revealed his glory, and his disciples believed in him. After this, he went down to Capernaum with his mother, brothers, and his disciples. They stayed there for a few days.

2:13-17 The First Journey to Jerusalem and cleansing of the temple- When it was almost time for the Jewish Passover, Jesus went up to Jerusalem. In the temple courts he found people selling cattle, sheep, doves, and others sitting at tables exchanging money. Jesus scattered the coins of the money changers and overturned their tables. He says to get these things out of here and to stop turning his Father's house into a market.

2:18-25 Jesus Predicts His Resurrection- The Jews question Jesus and ask him what sign he can show them to prove his authority to do all this. Jesus responds by saying to destroy the temple and he will raise it again in three days. They reply by saying it took forty-six years to build the temple, and questioned how Jesus will rebuild it in three days. But Jesus was referring to his body and predicted his own death and resurrection. After he was raised from the dead, the disciples remembered what Jesus had said here, then they believed the scripture and the words Jesus had spoken. While he was in Jerusalem at the Passover festival, many people saw the signs he was performing and believed in his name. But Jesus would not entrust himself to them, for he knew all people. He did not need any testimony about mankind because he knew what was in each person.

3:1-21 The Conversation with Nicodemus- There was a pharisee, a man named Nicodemus who was a member of the Jewish ruling council. He came to Jesus at night and said, "Rabbi we know that you are a teacher from God because no one could perform the signs you are doing unless God is with him." Jesus tells Nicodemus that no one can see the kingdom of God unless they are born again. Nicodemus said surely he cannot enter a mother's womb a second time to be born again. Jesus answered saying no one can enter the kingdom of God unless they are born of water and spirit, flesh gives birth to flesh, but spirit gives birth to spirit. Jesus tells him he should not be surprised at him saying that one must be born again. The wind blows wherever it pleases, you hear its sound but cannot tell where it comes from or where it is going, so it is with everyone born of the spirit. Nicodemus asked how this can be, and Jesus tells

Nicodemus he is Israel's teacher he should understand these things. People speak of what they know and testify what they have seen, but people will still not accept his testimony. If Jesus speaks of earthly things and they do not believe, how can he speak of heavenly things. Noone has ever gone into heaven except the one who came from heaven, the son of man. Just as Moses lifted up the snake in the wilderness, so the son of man must be lifted up, so that everyone who believes may have eternal life in him. For God so loved the world that he gave his one and only begotten son, that whoever believes in him shall not perish but have eternal life. God did not send his son into the world to condemn the world, but to save the world through him. Whoever believes in him is not condemned, but whoever does not believe stands condemned already because they have not believed in the name of God's one and only son. Light has come into the world, but people loved darkness instead of light because their deeds were evil. Everyone who does evil hates the light and will not come into the light for fear that their deeds will be exposed. But whoever lives by the truth comes into the light, so that it may be seen plainly that what they have done has been done in the sight of God.

3:22- 36 Jesus' Ministry in Judea and John's Testimony to Christ- After this, Jesus and his disciples went out into the Judean countryside. John the Baptist was near Salim where people were coming and being baptized. An argument developed between some of John's disciples and a certain Jew over the matter of ceremonial washing. John said that a person can receive only what is given to them from heaven. John says the one who comes from heaven is above all and affirms Jesus' glory and divine origin. He happily accepts his role in preparing the way for Jesus and declares that those who believe in Jesus have eternal life, while those who reject him face God's wrath.

4:4-26 The Conversation with the Woman of Samaria- Jesus had to go through Samaria because the pharisees heard he was gaining and baptizing more than John, but it was not even Jesus who baptized, it was his disciples. Jesus came to a town in Samaria called Sychar, near the plot of ground Jacob had given to his son Joseph. At noon, Jesus sat down by Jacobs well, since he was tired from the journey. A Samaritan woman came to draw water, and Jesus spoke to her and asked for a drink. Jesus disciples were in town to buy food at the time. The woman told Jesus she was a Samaritan, and he is a Jew, how can he ask her for a drink because Jews and Samaritans do not associate. Jesus told her if she only knew the gift of God and who she was talking to, then she would be the one asking for water and he would have given her living water. The woman told Jesus he has nothing to draw water with, how is he supposed to get this "living water." She asked him if he was greater than their father Jacob, the one who created the well and drank from it himself. Jacob's sons and livestock drank from it too. Jesus said that everyone who drinks from this well will become thirsty again. Whoever drinks the water from Jesus will never be thirsty again and will have eternal life. The woman said she wanted this water, so she will not get thirsty and have to keep coming back to draw water. Jesus told her to get her husband and come back, but the woman said she does not have a husband. Jesus knew this and proceeded to tell her personal details about her life so she could see he was a prophet. Jesus told her a time is coming and has now come when the true worshipers will worship the Father in the spirit and in truth, they are the kind of worshipers the Father seeks. God is spirit, and his worshipers must worship in the spirit and in truth. The woman told Jesus she knows that there will be a time when the messiah comes, and he will explain everything. Then Jesus declared "I, the one speaking to you, I am he."

4:27-42 The Disciples rejoin Jesus, and Samaritans start to believe- The disciples return and were surprised to find Jesus talking with a woman, but no one asked. They came out of the town and made their way toward him. The disciples urged Jesus to eat something, but Jesus said he has food they know nothing about yet. The disciples were talking to each other and said, "no one brought Jesus some food?" Jesus said his food is to do the will of the one who sent him and to finish his work. The disciples asked Jesus about one of his sayings about a harvest, Jesus told them the saying about how one sows, and another reaps is true. Both the Sower and the reaper are essential contributions to the harvest; each role carries significance and purpose. The Samaritan woman went back into town and told everyone about her encounter with Jesus and started asking if this could be the messiah. Many of the Samaritans from that town believed in him because of the woman's testimony, she told them about how Jesus knew everything she ever did. When the Samaritans came to Jesus, they urged him to stay with them. Jesus stayed with them for two days and his words made many more become believers. They already believed the woman, but now after hearing Jesus for themselves, they were saying wow he really is the savior of the world.

5:1-15 Healing at the Pool Second Journey (to Jerusalem) - Jesus went up to Jerusalem for one of the Jewish festivals. In Jerusalem near the sheep gate, which in Aramaic is called Bethesda. The pool is surrounded by five columns or colonnades. Many disabled people would hang around and lie there, the blind, lame, and paralyzed. There was a man who was invalid for thirty-eight years and when Jesus saw him lying there and learned he was in this condition for a long time, he asked the man if he would like to get well. The man replied and said every time he tries to get in the pool someone cuts him off and goes in front of him. Jesus tells him to pick up his mat and walk, instantly he was cured and walked. This encounter took place on the sabbath, and a Jewish leader went up to the man who had been healed and told him the law says it is forbidden to carry his mat on this day. The man replies and says he was told to carry his mat by the man who healed him. They asked him who this man was and who healed him. He did not know who healed him because Jesus had slipped away from the crowd that was there. Later Jesus found him at the temple and said it is good to see that he is well again, but to stop sinning or something worse could happen to him. The man who was healed went away and told the Jewish leaders it was Jesus who had made him well. (In the King James Bible, it gives more context as to why sick people lay at the pool. It says from time to time an angel of the lord would stir up the waters that would occasionally cure people.)

5:16-30 Jesus' Claims about His Authority and Unity with God- Since Jesus was doing these things on the Sabbath, the Jewish leaders began to harass him. Jesus was defending himself and told them that the Father is always at work to this very day, and he too is working. This response gave them all the reason more to kill him because he was not only breaking the sabbath but calling God his Father implying that he is equal to God. Jesus proceeds to tell them that the son can do nothing by himself, he can only do what he sees his Father doing. Whatever the Father does, the son also does. The Father loves the son and shows him all he does, and yes, he will show him even greater works than these. He says they will be amazed. The Father raises the dead and gives them life; the son gives life to whom he chooses and is pleased to give it. The Father judges no one and has entrusted all judgement to the son. All that honor the son also honor the Father. Whoever does not honor the son does not honor the Father, who sent him. Whoever hears his word and believes he who sent him has eternal life and will not be judged; they have crossed over from death to life. A time is coming and has come when the dead will hear the voice of Jesus and those who hear will live. The Father has life in himself, so he granted the son to also have life in himself. He has given the son of man authority to judge. Do not be amazed by this because a time is coming when all who are in their graves will hear his voice. Those who have done what is good will rise to live, and those who have done what is evil will rise to be condemned. His judgement is just, and he seeks to please the one who sent him. Jesus declares his unity with the Father, asserting that he only does what he sees the Father doing.

5:31-47 The Testimonies about Jesus- Jesus said that if he were to testify about himself then it would not be true, there are others who testify in his favor. Then they will know the testimony is true. John has been sent to testify to the truth, not that he needs or accepts human testimony, he mentions it so they may be saved. John was a lamp that burned and gave light, but Jesus has a testimony heavier than that of John. It is the works of the Father that was given to Jesus to finish, the very works he is doing, testify that the Father has sent him. The Father that has sent Jesus himself, and testified concerning Jesus. He tells the unbelievers that they study scriptures diligently because they think there is eternal life within them, but do not see that those very scriptures they study are testifying about Jesus. They refuse to come to him for life and do not believe the one the Father sent, so the word does not dwell in them. Jesus wonders why they believe they will accept glory from one another, but not seek the glory that only comes from God. Jesus tells them do not think that he will accuse them before the Father, their accuser is Moses, the one who their hopes are set on. Jesus said that if they believe Moses, then they should believe him because Moses wrote about him. So, if they do not believe what Moses wrote, how can they believe what Jesus says.

6:26-59 The Bread of Life (in Capernaum)- The crowd finds Jesus in Capernaum where he introduces himself as the bread of life, teaching that whoever comes to him will never go hungry or thirsty, and whoever believes in him will have eternal life. This teaching causes disputes and questions among the crowd. A crowd was looking for Jesus and they found him on the other side of the lake. Jesus tells them to not work for food that will spoil, but for food that endures to eternal life, which will be given by the son of man. God the Father has placed his seal of approval. They ask him what they must do to fulfill the work that God requires, Jesus answered saying that the work of God required is to believe in the one God has sent. They ask Jesus what signs to look out for when believing in him, he tells them that the Father is the one who gives the true bread from heaven, not Moses. Jesus told them the bread of God is the bread that comes down from heaven and gives life to the world. They ask him to give them this bread, and Jesus tells them that he is the bread of life. Whoever comes to him will never go hungry, and whoever believes in him will never be thirsty. He will never drive away those who come to him, he has come down from heaven for the will of God. He will not lose the ones given to him; he will raise up the ones who believe. Some of the Jews began to grumble saying they know Jesus' Father is Joseph and Mary, asking how he can he refer to his Father as God, and how he calls himself the bread that came down from heaven. Jesus tells them to stop grumbling among themselves and no one can come to him unless the Father draws them, they will raised up in the last days. Jesus repeats that he is the bread of life and whoever believes will have eternal life, no one has seen the Father except the ones who are from God. Everyone who has heard the Father and learned from him comes to Jesus. Ancestors ate food in the wilderness and now they are dead, he is offering bread that comes directly from heaven which anyone can eat and not die. Jesus is the living bread that came down from heaven. Whoever eats this bread will live forever. This bread is his flesh, which he will give for the life of the world. The Jews debate and argue among themselves how Jesus could literally offer them his flesh to eat. Jesus tells them whoever does not eat his flesh and drink his blood will have no life in them. His flesh is real food, and his blood is a real drink, whoever consumes it has him in them. Jesus lives just like the living Father does, so whoever feeds on him will live because of him. The bread is from heaven and eternal life is available for those who choose to eat it. All this was said while teaching in a synagogue in Capernaum.

6:60-66 Some followers desert Jesus- After hearing about eating flesh and drinking blood, some disciples grumble that this teaching is too hard to accept. Jesus asked if they are offended by this, and clarifies his words were not meant to be taken literally like a cannibal. He says the spirit gives life and the flesh counts for nothing. The words he speaks are full of spirit and life, yet some do not believe. This is why he says no one can come to him unless the Father has enabled them. At this point many followers turned back and no longer followed him. Jesus asked the twelve if they want to leave too, Simon Peter answers for the group and says no because they have come to believe and to know the Jesus is the holy one of God.

7:1-13 Jesus Remains in Galilee and goes to the Festival of Tabernacles- Jesus' brothers taunt him and do not believe in his divinity at first. Then he travels secretly to Jerusalem for the feast of tabernacles. Jesus tells his brothers that his time has not come yet, and about the world's coming hatred towards him. No one would speak up publicly about Jesus due to fear of the leaders.

7:14-24 Jesus Teaches at the Festival- Halfway through the festival, Jesus begins teaching openly in the temple courts, astonishing the Jews with his knowledge. They were amazed and asked how it is possible this man has so much knowledge without being taught. Jesus tells them the knowledge comes from the one who sent him and anyone who seeks God can see where his teachings come from. Whoever speaks for their own personal gain or glory, they speak on their own. If one seeks the glory of God, that is a person of truth and there is nothing false about them. Jesus confronts their misunderstanding and misjudgments, declaring that his authority comes from the one who sent him. He asked the crowd why they are trying to kill him and accuses them of not keeping the laws Moses gave. They respond by telling Jesus he is demon possessed and ask who is trying to kill him. Jesus criticizes them for being mad that he healed on the sabbath. They circumcise boys on the sabbath to uphold laws of Moses, but criticize Jesus for healing an entire body on that day. He told them to stop judging based off mere appearances, but instead judge correctly.

7:25-44 Division Over Who Jesus Is- Jesus' statements cause division among the crowd. Some believe he is the Christ, while others doubt because they know where he comes from, not realizing his divine origin. Some of the people in Jerusalem started to talk among themselves and ask, "isn't this the man they are trying to kill, here he is speaking publicly, and they are not saying a word to him, have they really concluded that he is the messiah?" The scriptures state that when the messiah comes, no one will know where he is from, so it made them wonder because they knew where he was from. Jesus was still teaching in the temple courts and said yes, they know him, and they know where he is from, he is here on the authority of the one who sent him. Jesus said he knows God because he is from him and was sent by him. After hearing this they tried to seize Jesus, but no one laid a hand on him because his time and hour had not come yet. Many in the crowd believed him, and when the chief priests and pharisees heard the whispers about Jesus, they ordered the temple guards to arrest him. However, Jesus continues to teach about his departure and where he will go, which further confuses the crowd. Jesus tells them he is only with them for a short time because he is going to the one who sent him. When they look for him, they will not find him because where he is going, they cannot come. The Jews start questioning what these words mean and why they will not be able to find him. They process the words from a human perspective and keep taking him literally, wondering if he means a different country like Greece when he said they will not find him where he is going. On the last day of the festival, Jesus invites anyone who is thirsty to come to him and drink. Whoever believes in him, rivers of living water will flow within them. The water represents the spirit, which believers will receive. This is the first time God's spirit has been given to humanity, so they are yet to understand what Jesus was referring to. There was still debate among the crowd regarding Jesus' divinity, some say he is a prophet while others are still skeptical how the messiah can come from Gallie, because it is written the messiah will come from the descendants of David and come from the town Bethlehem where David lived. The people were divided because of Jesus, but no one laid a hand on him.

7:45-53 Unbelief of the Jewish Leaders- The guards return without arresting Jesus because they were in awe over his words. When the chief priests and pharisees ask why they did not arrest Jesus, the guards say because no one has ever spoke the way this man does. The leaders respond to the guards telling them they were deceived too. The pharisees rebuke the guards and Nicodemus for their foolishness, deepening the division among the Jewish leaders. Nicodemus was a pharisee who believed in Jesus, he asked the leaders "since when does their law condemn men without hearing and finding out about them first?" The leaders sarcastically respond to Nicodemus asking if he is from Galilee too, that if he wants to look at the scripture he will see the messiah does not come from Galilee. The crowd dispersed after Jesus' teaching.

8:1-11 The Woman Caught in Adultery- Jesus appeared again in the temple courts and when the people gathered around him, he sat down to teach them. He was interrupted by the pharisees who brought in a woman caught for adultery. They made her stand before the group. They test Jesus by asking if she should be stoned because the law of Moses commanded them to do so. They thought they trapped Jesus with this trick question, so they could have an excuse to accuse him. Jesus bent down and started to write on the ground with his finger. He straightened up and declared, let any one of you who is without sin cast the first stone at her. Then he stooped down and began writing on the ground again. The people were conflicted by their consciences and their own lack of perfection. So they started to go away and dropped the stones from their hands one by one, starting with the elders until it was just Jesus and the woman left standing there. Jesus straightened up and asked the woman where everyone was and if anyone had condemned her. She responds to Jesus saying no one condemned her, then Jesus said he will not condemn her either and for her to go now and leave her life of sin.

8:12-20 "I am the Light of the World" Dispute Over Jesus' Testimony- Jesus spoke to the people again and declared that he is the light of the world. Whoever follows him will never walk in darkness and will have the light of life. The pharisees challenged him by saying his testimony is invalid because he cannot appear as his own witness. Jesus told them that even if he were to testify on his own behalf, his testimony would be valid because he knows where he came from and where he is going. He told the pharisees they have no idea about this, and they pass judgments based off human standards. Jesus does not pass judgements on people like the pharisees do. If he does judge, his decisions are true because he is not alone and stands with the Father. He told them their law is written; it says there needs to be two witnesses for a testimony to be valid. Jesus tells them he testifies for himself, and his other witness is the Father who sent him. Then they ask Jesus where his Father is, Jesus told them they do not know about him or the Father. If they knew him, they would know the Father also. He spoke these words by the temple courts where the offerings are put, yet no one seized him because his hour had not come yet.

8:21-29 Discussion with the Jews- Jesus says that when he goes away and they look for him, they will not find him and cannot go where he goes. The Jews misunderstood what these statements meant and asked if he is planning to kill himself. Jesus clarified by saying that they are from below and he is from above, they are of this world, and he is not. Jesus predicts his death and tells them again they will die in their sins if they do not believe in him. Jesus emphasizes his divine origin since the beginning, but some still do not believe or confused about what he is telling them about the Father. He confirms the trustworthiness of the Father who sent him. Jesus said when the son of man is lifted up, they will know that he is the one. He does nothing on his own and speaks what the Father taught him. The one who sent him is with him, he has not been left alone and always does what pleases him. As he spoke, many believed in him.

8:31-36 "The Truth will Set You Free" - Jesus tells the Jews who believe in him, if they hold his teaching, they are his disciples. They will know truth, and the truth will set them free. They do not understand and tell Jesus that Abraham's descendants are not slaves of anyone, so how can they be set free. Jesus tells them that everyone who sins is a slave to sin. A slave has no permanent place in a family, if the son of the family set the slave free, then they would indeed be free.

8:37-47 Children of the Devil-The Jews take offense, leading to a debate about their spiritual ancestry, with Jesus asserting their actions align more with the devil than Abraham. Jesus tells them he knows they are Abraham's descendants, yet they are looking for a way to kill him, because they have no room for his word. He is telling them what he has seen in the Fathers presence. Jesus accuses them of not being Abraham's children because they are not doing what Abraham would have. He told them they are plotting to kill him, and Abraham would not plot such evil things, especially to a man who has told them truth from God. The pharisees protested and told Jesus they are not illegitimate children and the only Father they have is God. Jesus tells them if God were their Father, they would love him, because he came here from God. He said he has not come on his own, God sent him. Jesus asked them why his language is not clear to them and why they are unable to hear what he is saying. Then he tells them they belong to the devil, because they only want to carry out the desires of the devil. He has been a murderer from the beginning and never truthful. The devil is the father of lies and when he lies, he speaks his native language. Jesus tells them truth, but they do not believe. Nobody can prove Jesus guilty of one sin and only speaks truth. Whoever belongs to God can understand and hear him, the reason they do not hear is because they do not belong to God.

8:48- 59 Before Abraham was, I am - The Jews insult Jesus by asking him if they are right in saying that he is a Samaritan and demon possessed. Jesus tells them a demon does not possess him; he honors his Father, but they dishonor him. He says he is not seeking glory for himself but there is one who seeks it, and he is the judge. Whoever obeys his words will never see death. After hearing these words, they exclaimed that now they know for sure he is demon possessed because Abraham died and so did the other prophets, yet Jesus claims that whoever obeys his words will never taste death. They ask Jesus if he is greater than their father Abraham because Abraham died. Then they ask Jesus who does he think he is, making such claims. Jesus says that if he glorifies himself, it means nothing, His Father, who they claim as their God is the one who glorifies him. Jesus told them he knows the Father, and they do not, If Jesus said he did not know the Father, then he would be a liar like them, but he does know him and obeys his word. He tells them that Abraham rejoiced at the thought of seeing his day, he saw it and was glad. The Jews do not believe Jesus and say he is not even fifty years old, how could he have seen Abraham, that ridiculous. Jesus proclaims that before Abraham was born, he was. That statement is basically claiming to be God if Jesus says he was alive before Abraham. At this, they picked up stones to throw at him, but Jesus slipped away from the temple grounds.

9:1-7 Jesus Heals a Man Born Blind- Jesus and his disciples encounter a man blind from birth. The disciples question whether the man or his parents sin caused his blindness. Jesus refutes this and states the man's blindness is to display God's works. He then heals the man using a mixture of saliva and dirt, instructing him to wash in the Pool of Siloam.

9:8-12 The blind man's testimony- People familiar with the blind man debate whether it is the same person who was healed, and whether it is the same guy who used to sit and beg. Some claim it was the same person and others said it just looked like the same person, refusing to believe it. The healed man insists he is the same person and testifies about Jesus' miracle.

9:13-34 The Pharisees Investigate the Healing- The Pharisees investigate the miracle, split over its implications due to its occurrence on the sabbath. The pharisees ask the man how he received his sight, the man responds by saying mud was put in his eyes, then he washed, and now he can see. Some of the pharisees said this man is not from God because he does not keep the sabbath, but others question how a sinner can perform such signs, so they were divided. They turned to the blind man again and asked his opinions about Jesus. The man tells them Jesus is a prophet. The pharisees were still not believing it and sent for the man's parents, to get further confirmation of this guy's legitimacy. They ask the parents if this man is their son, if he was born blind, and how is it that he can see. The parents confirm it is their son, and he was born blind, but they do not know how he can see or who opened his eyes. The parents were afraid of the Jewish leaders because they already threatened expulsion from the synagogue for anyone who acknowledges that Jesus is the messiah. So, the parents refrained from saying anything more and told the pharisees their son is of age and to ask him these questions, he can speak for himself. They summoned the blind man a second time and the man bravely defends Jesus, resulting in his expulsion from the synagogue.

9:35-41 Spiritual Blindness- Jesus heard they had thrown him out and finds the expelled man. Jesus reveals his identity as the son of man and tells the man he is in fact speaking with him. The man confesses his faith in Jesus. Jesus talks about spiritual blindness saying that he has come into this world for judgement, so the blind may see. The pharisees who were with him heard this and asked if they were blind too. Jesus tells them they would not be guilty of sin if they were blind, but the fact they claim they can see, their guilt remains.

10:1-21 "I am the Good Sheperd"- The good shepherd and his sheep are a metaphor for the relationship between Jesus and his followers. Jesus, as the good shepherd, guides, provides, and protects his sheep. He also lays down his life for them, unlike the hired shepherd who abandons them when danger comes. The sheep know and trust the good shepherd and follow his voice. Jesus tells the pharisees that anyone who does not enter the sheep pen by the gate and climbs in some other way is a thief and a robber. The one who enters by the gate is the shepherd of the sheep. The gatekeeper opens the gate for him, and the sheep listen to his voice. He calls his sheep out by name and leads them out. His sheep follow him because they know his voice. They will never follow a stranger because they do not recognize a stranger's voice. The pharisees do not understand the parable. Jesus says that he is the gate for the sheep. All that come before him are thieves and robbers, but the sheep have not listened to them. He is the gate, whoever enters through him will be saved. They will come in and go out and find pasture. The thief comes only to steal, kill, and destroy. Jesus has come so that they may have life, and have it to the full. Jesus is the good shepherd, and the good shepherd lays down his life for the sheep. The hired help is not the shepherd and does not own the sheep, so when they see a wolf coming, they will abandon the sheep and run away. Then the wolf attacks the flock and scatters it. The man runs away because he is hired help and does not care about the sheep. Jesus is the good shepherd, he knows his sheep and the sheep know him. The same way the Father knows him, and he knows the Father, he lays down his life for the sheep. He has other sheep too that are not of this sheep pen, he must bring them also. They too will listen to his voice and there shall be one flock and one shepherd. The reason the Father loves him is because he lays down his life, only to take it up again. No one takes it from him; he lays down his life on his terms. He has the authority to lay it down and authority to take it up again. This command he received from the Father. The Jews who heard these words were divided once again. They said he is demon possessed and raving mad, asking why they should listen to him. But others said these are not the sayings of a man who is possessed by a demon, a demon cannot open the eyes of the blind.

10:22-42 Jesus at the Feast of Dedication in Jerusalem and declares unity with the Father-It was winter, and it was the festival of dedication at Jerusalem. Jesus was in the temple courts walking in Solomon's colonnade and the Jews gathered around him. They ask Jesus how long he will keep them in suspense, and to just say it directly if he is the messiah. Jesus says he did tell them this already, but they do not believe. The works he does in his Father's name testify about him, but they do not believe it because they are not his sheep. Jesus knows his sheep; they listen to his voice and follow him. He gives them eternal life, and they shall never perish. No one will snatch them out of his hand. The Father who has given them to him is greater than all, no one can snatch them out of his Fathers hand. Jesus says that he and the Father are one. That is another statement of Jesus saying he is God. Once again, the Jewish opponents pick up stones to throw at him. Jesus tells them that he has shown them many good works from the Father and asks why they will stone him. They say they are not going to stone him for the good works; they will stone him because he is just a mere man, and it is blasphemy to claim to be God. Jesus tells them about the Father who set apart his very own to send into the world. He says to believe in the works of the Father so they may know and understand that the Father is in him, and he in the Father. They tried to seize him, but he escaped their grasp. Jesus went back across to Jordan to the same place where John had been baptizing in the early days. There he stayed, and people came to him saying that John spoke the truth even though he never performed a sign. In that place many came to believe in Jesus.

11:1-16 The Death of Lazarus-There was a man named Lazarus from Bethany, who was the brother of Mary and Martha. Lazarus falls sick and the sisters sent word to Jesus about his sickness. When Jesus heard this, he says that this sickness will not end in death, it is for God's glory that God's son may be glorified through it. Jesus loved Martha, her sister, and Lazarus, so when he heard Lazarus was sick, he stayed two more days. He told the disciples let us go back to Judea, but they were concerned about going back because the Jews just tried to stone him there not too long ago. Jesus says they will be fine because there is twelve hours of daylight and anyone who walks in the daytime will not stumble. He announces Lazarus's death to the disciples, and they will go to him so Jesus can wake him up.

11:16-37 Jesus Comforts the Sisters of Lazarus- When he arrives, Jesus finds out that Lazarus had already been in the tomb for four days. Bethany was a town in Judea that was less than two miles from Jerusalem, many Jews had already come to Martha and Mary to comfort them because of the loss of their brother. When Martha heard Jesus was coming, she went out to meet him. Jesus tells her that her brother will rise again, but she thought he meant in the last days not now. Jesus tells Martha that he is the resurrection and the life, the ones who believe in him will live, even though they die. He says whoever lives by believing in him will never die, then asks Martha if she believes this. Martha said yes lord, she believes that he is the messiah, the Son of God, the one who has come into this world. After she said this, she called her sister Mary and told her the teacher is here and asking for her. Mary heard this and quickly got up and went to him. There were Jews who were at Mary's house comforting her, they noticed how quickly she got up and went out. They followed her thinking she was going to visit the tomb to mourn there. Mary reached the place where Jesus was, she fell at his feet wishing he were there when her brother died. Mary was weeping and the Jews who followed her were also weeping. Jesus was deeply moved in spirit and troubled. He asked where the body is laid, and they told Jesus to follow them and see. They saw how moved Jesus was and pointed out how much he loved him, but some of them wondered how he could open the eyes of a blind man but not prevent Lazarus from dying.

11:38-44 Jesus Raises Lazarus From the Dead- Jesus, who was deeply moved came to the tomb and sees the cave with a stone laid across the entrance. He said to take away the stone. Martha tells Jesus that there will be a bad odor by this time because he had been there for four days. Jesus reminds her of what he said, that if she believes she will see the glory of God. They took away the stone, then Jesus looks up and thanked the Father for hearing him. He says that he knows that he always hears him, but this is for the benefit of the people standing here, so that they may believe that the Father sent him. Jesus called in a loud voice and said Lazarus, come out! The dead man came out with his hands and feet wrapped in strips of linen, and a cloth wrapped around his face. Jesus said to them, take off the grave clothes and let him go.

11:45-57 The Plot to Kill Jesus- The Jews who were at Mary's house who witnessed what happened to Lazarus believed in Jesus, they went to the pharisees to tell them what happened. Then the chief priests and the pharisees called a meeting of the Sanhedrin. They ask each other what they are accomplishing, they have a man here who is performing many signs. They said if they let Jesus go on like this, everyone will believe him. They were worried the romans will take away both their temple and their nation. Then one of them named Caiaphas, who was the high priest that year, spoke up and said they know nothing at all. He said they do not realize that it is better for them if one man dies for the people rather than the whole nation perish. As high priest that year, he prophesied that Jesus would die for the Jewish nation, and not only for that nation but also for the scattered children of God, to bring them together and make them one. There was irony in Caiaphas' statement, and the high priest did not understand the ramifications of his own statement. Caiaphas prophecy intended one meaning but God another. So, from that day on they plotted to take Jesus' life. Therefore, Jesus no longer moved about publicly among the people of Judea. He withdrew to a region near the wilderness, to a village called Ephraim, where he stayed with his disciples. The chief priests and the pharisees had given orders that anyone who found out where Jesus was should report it so they can arrest him. They kept a lookout for Jesus at the temple courts and wondered if he was going to show up to the festival.

12:9-11 The Plot against Lazarus- A large crowd of Jews found out that Jesus was there and came, not only because of him but also to see Lazarus, whom he had raised from the dead. The chief priests made plans to kill Lazarus as well, because his testimony was causing many of the Jews to go over to Jesus and believe in him.

12:20-36 Greeks Seek Jesus; Jesus predicts his death- There were some Greeks who went up to worship at the festival, they came up to Phillip requesting to see Jesus. Phillip told Andrew, who in turn told Jesus. Jesus replied by saying that the hour has come for the son of man to be glorified. Jesus compares his death and resurrection to a kernel of wheat falling into the earth to produce many seeds. Anyone who loves their life will lose it, while anyone who hates their life in this world will keep it for eternal life. Whoever serves Jesus must follow him; and where he is, his servant will also be. His Father will honor the one who serves him.

12:37-50 The Belief and Unbelief of the People- Despite witnessing many signs, the Jews do not believe in Jesus. Jesus proclaims that he came not to judge but to save the world, and those who reject his words will be judged on the last day. This fulfilled the prophecy of Isaiah which said their eyes would blinded and their hearts hardened, so they cannot see with their eyes or understand with their hearts. Isaiah had seen the lord's glory and spoke about him in his time. God is set to judge the people, and they will not be healed. When he references people's hearts hardened and eyes blinded, it means they will not accept truth even after witnessing miracles. Yet at the same time, many even among the leaders believed in Jesus, but they could not openly acknowledge their faith because of the fear of the pharisees. They worried about being kicked out of the synagogue, for they loved human praise more than praise from God. Jesus cried out saying that whoever believes in him also believes in the one who sent him. He said whoever looks at him, is also seeing God. Jesus came into this world as a light so that the believers will not have to stay in darkness. If anyone hears his words and does not keep them, he will not judge. He came to save the world, not judge it. There is a judge for the ones who reject him and do not accept his words, the very words he has spoken will condemn them at the last day. Jesus does not speak on his own, the Father who sent him commanded him to say all that he has spoken. He said he knows that his command leads to eternal life, so whatever he says is just what the Father has told him to say.

13:31-35 A New Commandment of Love- After Judas left, Jesus said the son of man is now glorified and God is glorified in him. If God is glorified in him, God will glorify the son in himself and will glorify him at once. Jesus refers to his disciples as his children and tells them that he will only be with them for a little longer. He said they will look for him, same thing he told the Jews; where he is going, they cannot come. Jesus gave them a new command which is to love one another, just as he has loved them. They must love one another and by this everyone will know that they are his disciples.

14:1-4 Jesus Comforts His Disciples- Jesus tells the disciples to not let their hearts be troubled. Since they believe in God, they also believe in him. Jesus says his house has many rooms, that he would not have told them he is going there unless he had prepared a place for them. He said if he prepares a place for them, he will come back and take them to be with him and be where he is. Jesus states that they know where he is going, Thomas responds and says that he does not know where he is going.

14:5-14 Jesus the Way to the Father- Thomas questions Jesus about where he is going, and Jesus explains his unity with the Father. Thomas asked Jesus, if they do not know where he is going, how can they know the way. Jesus states that he is the way, the truth, and the life. No one comes to the Father except through him. Jesus says if they really know him, then they will know the Father as well and that from now on, they do know him and have seen him. Phillip asks Jesus to just show them the Father and that will be enough for them. Jesus asks Phillip how can he say "show them the Father" because anyone who has seen him has seen the Father. He asks Phillip how he does not know him by now, even after he has been among them for such a long time. Does he not believe that he is in the Father, and the Father in him. Jesus says that the words he says to them is not on his own authority. It is from the Father, who is living in him, who is doing his work. Believe him when he says that he is in the Father, and the Father in him; or at least believe the evidence of the works themselves. Very truly he says, whoever believes in him will do the works he has been doing. They will do even greater things than these because Jesus is going to the Father. He will do whatever they ask in his name, so that the Father may be glorified in the son. He says that they may ask anything in his name, and he will do it.

14:15-26 Jesus Promises the Holy Spirit- Jesus promises to send the holy spirit, which is also called the advocate, to help and be with his followers. Jesus says if you love him, then keep his commands. Jesus will ask the Father to give them another advocate to help them and be with them forever. The advocate that Jesus is talking about is the spirit of truth. The world cannot accept it yet because they have neither seen him nor know him. He lives with the disciples, and he will be in them. Jesus says he will not leave them as orphans; he will come to them. He tells them in the near future the world will not see him anymore, but they will see him because he lives, they will also live. On that day they will realize that he is in the Father, they are in him, and Jesus in them. Jesus says whoever has his commands and keeps them is the one who loves him. The one who loves him will be loved by his Father, and Jesus will love them and show himself to them. Judas the disciple (not Iscariot) asked the lord why he intends to show himself to them and not to the world. Jesus replied by saying that anyone who loves him will obey his teaching. His Father will love them; Jesus and his Father will come and make their home with them. Anyone who does not love him will not obey his teaching. These words that are heard are not his own; they belong to the Father who sent him. Jesus says all these things while he is still with them in flesh. The advocate, the holy spirit, whom the Father will send in his name, will teach them all the things and remind them of everything he said to them.

14:27-31 The Gift of Peace, Final Teachings and Comfort- Jesus said he leaves them with peace and gives them peace, but does not give it to them in the same way the world gives. He tells them to not let their hearts be troubled and to not be afraid. Jesus reminds them of what they heard him say, that he is going away and then coming back to them. If they loved him, they would be glad he is going to the Father, for the Father is greater than him. Jesus tells them now before it happens so that when it does happen, they will believe. He said that he will not say much more to them, for the prince of this world is coming who has no hold over him. Jesus is referring to the prince of this world as Satan. Jesus is aware of his impending attack and is confident that Satan has no power over him. He comes so that the world may learn that he loves the Father and does exactly what the Father has commanded him. Jesus tells the disciples to come now and they leave.

15:1-8 Jesus the True Vine- Jesus says that he is the true vine, and his Father is the gardener or the vineyard keeper. He cuts off every branch in him that bears no fruit, while every branch that does bear fruit, he cleanses so that it will be even more fruitful. Jesus tells them they are already clean because of the words he has spoken to them. Remain in him, as he remains in them. No branch can bear fruit by itself, it must remain in the vine. Neither can they bear fruit unless they remain in him. Jesus is the vine, and the disciples are the branches. If they remain in him and him in them, they will bear much fruit; apart from him they can do nothing. If they do not remain in him, they are like a branch that is thrown away and withers; such branches are picked up and thrown into the fire to be burned. If they remain in him and his words remain in them, ask for whatever and it will be done. This is to his Fathers glory, so they may bear much fruit, showing themselves to be his disciples.

15:9-17 Abiding in Love- As the Father loved Jesus, he loves them. He says to remain in his love. If they keep his commands, they will remain in his love, just as Jesus kept his Fathers commands and remains in his love. He tells them this so that his joy may be in them, and so their joy may be complete. His command is this; love each other as Jesus loves them. He says greater love is to lay down one's life for a friend, Jesus calls them his friends if they do what he commands. He no longer calls them servants because a servant does not know the business of his master. Instead, he calls them friends because everything he learned from the Father has been made known to them. They did not choose Jesus; he chose them and appointed them so that they may go bear fruit that will last. Whatever is asked in his name, the Father will give. This is his command: to love each other.

15:18-25 The World's Hatred-Jesus warns his disciples that they will face persecution from the world because they are not of the world. He points out that their persecution is due to the world's hatred of him. Jesus says that if the world hates them, keep in mind they hated him first. If they belonged to the world, it would love them. Jesus says that he chooses them out of this world, which is why the world hates them. When they treat them this way in Jesus name, they do not know the one who sent him. Jesus said if he had not come and spoken to them, they would not be guilty of sin, but now they have no excuse for their sin. Whoever hates Jesus, hates the Father as well. If he had not done the works among them no one else did, they would not be guilty of sin. But they have seen, and still chose to hate both him and the Father. This is fulfilled what is written in their law which prophesied "They hated me without reason."

15:26-27 The Witness of the Holy Spirit- Jesus tells them the advocate will come, whom he will send to them from the Father. The advocate is the spirit of truth who goes out from the Father, he will testify about him. Also, they must testify since they have been with Jesus from the beginning.

16:1-4- The Work of the Holy Spirit- Jesus warns his disciples about the impending persecution they will face, he tells them all this so they will not fall away. He says they will be thrown out of the synagogues, and a time will come when their persecutors think they are offering a service to God by killing them. They will do such things because they do not know the Father or him. Jesus tells them these things so that when their time comes, they will remember that he warned them about the persecutors.

16:5-15 The Work of the Holy Spirit- Jesus points out that none of them ask him where he is going when he says that he is going to him who sent him. Rather, they are filled with grief because he has said these things. Jesus tells the disciples it is truly a good thing that he is going away. The holy spirit cannot come to them unless he goes away. When Jesus goes, he will send the advocate to them. When he comes, he will prove the world to be in the wrong about sin, righteousness, and judgement. The holy spirit will guide them into all the truth and convict the world of sin. It will glorify Jesus by receiving and declaring what is his. The prince of this world now stands condemned in judgement. Jesus said that he has much more to say to them, more than they can bear. When the spirit of truth comes, he will not speak on his own. He will speak only what he hears, and he will tell them what is yet to come. All that belongs to the Father is his, that is why he said the spirit will receive from him what he will make known to them. The holy spirit will reveal everything that the disciples need to know about Jesus, he will make it clear them.

16:16-25 Sorrow Turned to Joy- Some of the disciples said to one another they did not understand what Jesus meant when he said, "in a little while they will see him no more, then after a little while they will see him." Jesus saw that the disciples wanted to ask him about this, so he tells them about his brief departure and return, which will transform their sorrow into joy. He compares their situation to a woman in childbirth whose anguish turns into joy once the baby is born. Jesus says that now is their time of grief, but he will see them again and they will rejoice, and no one will take away their joy. He emphasizes that anything that is asked in the Father's name will be given to them. Jesus said they have not asked for anything in his name up until now. He told them ask, and they will receive, and their joy will be complete.

16:25-33 Prayer in the Name of Jesus, Overcome the World- Jesus says that although he has been speaking figuratively, there is a time coming when he will no longer use this kind of language. He will tell them plainly about his Father. On that day, they will ask in his name, and he is not saying that he will ask the Father on their behalf. No, the Father loves them because they loved Jesus and believed that he came from God. Jesus states that he came from the Father and entered the world, now he is leaving the world and going back to the Father. His disciples said, now he is speaking clearly without figures of speech. They said they can now see that Jesus knows all things, and he does not need to have anyone ask him questions. This makes them believe he came from God. Jesus asks them if they believe him now, a time is coming and has come when they will be scattered, each at their own home. They will leave him all alone, yet he is not alone, for the Father is with him. Jesus tells them these things, so that in him they may have peace. In this world they will have trouble but take heart because he has overcome the world.

17:1-5 Jesus Prays for Himself- Jesus looked up to heaven praying to the Father and said that the hour has come, to glorify his son, so that his son may glorify him. Jesus acknowledges his holy mission and the glory of the Father. He speaks of his authority over all humanity and his role in offering eternal life, bringing glory to the Father by finishing the works that he was given to do. Jesus asks the Father to glorify him in his presence with the glory he had with him before the world began.

17:6-19 Jesus Prays for His Disciples- Jesus shifts his prayer to his disciples, praying for their protection, unity, joy, and sanctification. Now they know with certainty that everything given to Jesus comes from God. They believe the Father sent Jesus, and that Jesus comes from God. Jesus gave them the words given to him by the Father and they accepted him. Jesus prays for his disciples, he is not praying for the world, but for those given to him from the Father. Jesus says he will not remain in the world any longer, but they are still in the world, and he is coming to the Father. He addresses the holy Father to protect them by the power of his name, the name he was given, so that they may know the Father and him are one. He tells the Father that he protected them and kept them safe while he was with them by the name he was given. None has been lost except the one doomed to destruction, so that the scripture would be fulfilled. Jesus tells the Father that he is coming to him now, and he says these things while still in the world so that they have the full measure of his joy within them. He has given them the Fathers word, and the world hated them, for they are not of the of this world any more than he is of this world. His prayer is not for the Father to take them out of this world; his prayer is for him to protect them from the evil one. They are not of this world, even as he is not of it. Jesus prays to sanctify them by the truth; his word is truth. Just as the Father sent him into the world, Jesus has sent them into the world. Jesus will sanctify himself for them, so that they too may be truly sanctified. Sanctify means to set apart, purify, or made holy.

17:20-26 Jesus Prays for All Believers- Jesus' prayer is not just for them alone, he also prays for those who will believe in him through the disciples' message. He prays that all of them may be one, just as the Father is with him, may he be in them. May the believer be in the Father and Jesus, so that the world may believe God sent Jesus. He has given believers the glory that the Father gave him, so they can be one, just as God and Jesus are one. Jesus within them, like the Father within Jesus, so that they may be brought to complete unity. Then the world will know that God sent him and has loved them, just as God loved him. Jesus asks the Father to be with those who were given to him, to see his glory, the glory given to him because he loved Jesus before the creation of the world. Jesus tells the righteous Father that even though the world does not know him, he knows him, and they know that the Father has sent him. Jesus has made God the Father known to them and will continue to make the Father known so that the love he has for Jesus may be in them and that he himself may be in them.

19:31-37 Fulfillment of Scripture, Jesus' Side Pierced- It was the day of preparation, and the next day was to be a special sabbath. The Jewish leaders did not want the bodies left on the crosses during the sabbath, so they request the breaking of the legs of those crucified to expedite their deaths. When they come to Jesus and find him already dead, they do not break his legs, fulfilling scripture. One of the soldiers pierced Jesus' side with a spear, bringing a sudden flow of blood and water, also fulfilling scripture. The man who saw it has given testimony, and his testimony is true. He knows that he tells the truth, and he testifies so that others may also believe.

20:24-29 Jesus and Thomas- Thomas was one of the twelve who was not with the disciples when Jesus first resurrected. Thomas refuses to believe until he can see and touch Jesus' wounds himself. The other disciples told him they had seen the resurrected lord. Thomas said he will not believe unless he sees the nail marks in his hands, and physically touch Jesus with his fingers and hands where the nails were and on the side where Jesus was pierced. Eight days later, Jesus appears again and said peace be with them, then tells Thomas to touch his wounds. Jesus tells Thomas to stop doubting and believe. Thomas believes and confesses Jesus as his lord and his God. Jesus tells him he believes because he has seen him, blessed are the ones who have not seen and yet still believe.

20:30-31 The Purpose of John's Gospel- Jesus performed many other signs in the presence of his disciples, which are not recorded in this book. These are written so that one may believe that Jesus is the messiah, the Son of God, and that one may have life in his name by believing.

21:1-14 Jesus and the Miraculous Catch of Fish- Afterward, Jesus appeared to his disciples by the sea of Galilee. This is how it happened, Simon Peter, Thomas (also known as Didymus), Nathanael from Cana in Galilee, the sons of Zebedee, and two other disciples were together. Simon Peter told them he is going out to fish, and they said they will go with him. They went out and got into the boat, but that night they caught nothing. Early in the morning Jesus stood there on the shore, but the disciples did not realize that it was Jesus. He called out to them and asked them if they got any fish, and they told him no. Jesus told them to throw their net on the right side of the boat, and they will find some. When they did, they were unable to pull the net in because of the large number of fish. A disciple who Jesus loved yelled out to Peter saying, "It is the Lord!" As soon as Peter heard that, he wrapped his outer garments around him and jumped into the water, the other disciples followed. They were not far from shore, about a hundred yards. When they landed they saw a fire of burning coals with fish on it and some bread. Jesus told them to bring some of the fish they just caught. Then Simon Peter climbed back into the boat and dragged the net ashore. The net was full of hundreds of large fish, but even with so many the net was still not torn. Jesus came back, took the bread, then the fish, and gave it to them. This was now the third time Jesus appeared to his disciples after he was raised from the dead.

21:15-19 Jesus Reinstates Peter- When they had finished eating, Jesus asks Peter three times if he loves him in a symbolic act mirroring Peter's previous denial. Each time Peter affirms his love, Jesus instructs him to feed his lambs and tend his sheep, signifying the pastoral role Peter will play. Jesus prophesies that Peter will die a martyr's death that will glorify God.

21:20-25: The Fate of John and Closing of the Gospel- Peter noticed John and started to wonder about his fate. Jesus told Peter to not worry about him and just follow the lord because Peter had a purpose to help lead the Jesus movement and church. John's purpose or job of his long life was to stand witness to all these things so that others may believe. This is the disciple who testifies to these things and who wrote them down. Jesus did many other things and if all of them were written down, there would not have enough room for the books that would be written.

Acts

The book Acts is a collection of writings that is connected to the gospel of Luke. It has the same author Luke and is the second half of his gospel. It follows what happens to Jesus' followers after his resurrection and how the spirit helps expand the good news of Jesus to the world. It shows how it spreads through Jerusalem first, then into the neighboring regions like Judea and Samaria, to Palestine, into Rome, into Europe, and the ends of the earth.

In chapter 1, Jesus goes up into heaven. The book of Acts begins by recounting Jesus' ministry and his instruction to the apostles he had chosen through the holy spirit. After his suffering, he presented himself to them and gave many convincing proofs that he was alive. Jesus appeared to them over a period of forty days and spoke about the kingdom of God. On one occasion while eating with them, Jesus gave a command to not leave Jerusalem and to wait for the gift his Father promised them, the gift which they have heard him speak about. John baptized with water, but in a few days, they will be baptized with the holy spirit. The apostles gather around Jesus, they ask if he is going to restore the kingdom to Israel. Jesus tells them it is not for them to know the times or dates the Father set by his own authority, but they will receive power from the holy spirit when it comes onto them. They will be his witnesses in Jerusalem, Judea, Samaria, and to the ends of the earth. After he said this, Jesus ascends into heaven before their very eyes and disappeared into the clouds. They were looking intently up into the sky when suddenly two men dressed in white stood beside them. The two men asked them why they stand there looking into the sky, and that Jesus will come back the same way they have seen him go into heaven.

Then the apostles returned to the Mount of Olives and when they arrived, they went upstairs to the room they were staying. Those present were Peter, John, James and Andrew; Philip and Thomas, Bartholomew and Matthew; James' son of Alphaeus and Simon the Zealot, and Judas son of James. They all joined together constantly in prayer, along with the women and Mary the mother of Jesus, and with his brothers. Peter stood up and addressees a group of believers, there were about a hundred and twenty of them. Peter says to his brothers and sisters, the scripture had to be fulfilled in which the holy spirit spoke long ago through David about Judas, who served as a guide for those who arrested Jesus. Judas was one of their own in their shared ministry, who ended up buying a field with the money he received for betraying the lord. He died a gruesome death that is described as falling headlong, and his body bursting open and intestines spilling out. Everyone in Jerusalem heard about what happened to Judas and called it the field of blood. Peter says that it is written in the book of Psalms for another take his place of leadership. Therefore, it is necessary to choose one of them who has been with them since the beginning. They nominate two men who have been with them since Jesus was living among them, from the beginning during Johns baptism to the time when Jesus ascended. One of them must become a witness of his resurrection. The two nominated names of the men were, Barsabbas (also known as Justus) and Matthias. They prayed to the lord and stated that God knows everyone's hearts, show them which of these two he has chosen to take over this apostolic ministry which Judas left. Then they cast lots, and the lot fell to Matthias so, he was added to the eleven apostles.

In chapters 2-7, The holy spirit guides the apostles to spread the good news of Jesus and establish a church in Jerusalem first. **In chapter 2,** they were all together in one place for

Pentecost and suddenly a sound like the blowing of a violent wind came from heaven and filled the whole house where they were sitting. They saw tongues of fire that separated and came to rest on each of them. They were able to speak in other languages they did not know, and the people gathered there understood. All of them were filled with the holy spirit, which enabled them to speak in each other's tongues. The multicultural crowd was bewildered because they were hearing their native languages. People were amazed wondering what it meant, while others suggest they had too much wine. God's glory and this moment where his spirit is poured out is prophesied in the Old Testament. In the Chronicles, the Israelites saw the fire coming down and the glory of the lord filled the temple. In Haggai, it says the lord will fill the house with glory to all the nations. He refers to the prophet Joel, who said God will pour out his spirit on all people, allowing them to prophesy. He uses Psalms to demonstrate that David spoke about the resurrection of Christ. Also, Ezekiel showed the spirit and glory of the lord filling the temple. It is written that the lord's spirit will reside in the new messianic kingdom. God promised in the Old testament that he will live by his spirit with his people in the new temple. God's fiery presence is poured out and dwells in his people. Luke is saying that the new temple promised by the prophets is Jesus' new covenant family. Luke goes into detail of all the different races, tribes, and cultures who will have their hearts transformed by declaring Jesus as both the lord and the messiah. Peter instructs them to repent and be baptized in the name of Jesus Christ for the forgiveness of sins, and they will receive the holy spirit. The new believers devote themselves to the apostles' teaching, fellowship, breaking of bread, and prayer.

In chapter 3, Peter and John encounter a disabled man begging, and Peter heals the man in the name of Jesus. The miraculous healing causes astonishment and large crowds to gather around Peter and John. Peter uses this opportunity to preach about Jesus, repentance, and future judgement. He demonstrated the power of faith in Jesus, and the importance of salvation through belief and repentance.

In chapter 4, Peter and John get questioned and arrested. The Jewish leaders did not want them talking about Jesus or his resurrection, and despite attempts to silence them, they boldly proclaim that salvation can only be found in Jesus. Believers meet at Solomon's Colonnade in the temple courts, and increasingly more men and women believe in the lord. They share everything they have, sell property and possessions to give to anyone who is in need. They meet daily, break bread in homes, and eat with glad and sincere hearts, praising God and accepting favor with all the people. The religious leaders order them to stop speaking in Jesus' name, and eventually Peter and John are released from jail.

In chapter 5, there is a husband and wife called Ananias and Sapphira who sold a piece of property and lied about giving the proceeds to the church. Peter exposes the deception and highlights the authority of the church, and both of them were struck dead. The story emphasizes the importance of honesty and integrity, and that God is the ultimate judge who is aware of all hidden actions. The apostles continue to preach and perform miracles which draws the attention of Jewish authorities who arrest and put them in jail. But an angel of the lord opens the prison doors to release them so they can continue to preach. The authorities discover their escape and arrest them again, bringing them to Sanhedrin. Peter confidently declares that they must obey God over men, and a respected pharisee suggests that if it is a man-made religion, then it will die on its own. They listened to that councils advice and released them, but orders them to stop speaking in Jesus name. The apostles rejoice that they are worthy to suffer for Jesus, and of course they never stopped teaching and proclaiming the good news that Jesus is messiah.

In chapter 6, several widows reported that they were overlooked in the daily food distribution. This led to the twelve meeting and deciding to select seven men whose responsibility it will be to distribute the food to all the growing number of believers. The twelve did this because they wanted to give their attention to the ministry of the word of God full time and not neglect. They made sure the food distributers were good men full of the holy spirit and wisdom. After the seven men were selected, the apostles prayed and laid their hands on them, officially appointing them as deacons. One of the seven men selected was named Stephen, he was full of God's grace and power. The Jewish leaders felt threatened by Stephen's preaching and were unable to counter the wisdom given to him by the spirit as he spoke. This opposition resorted to false accusations, claiming he spoke blasphemous words against Moses and against God. They stirred up the people, the elders, and teachers of law which led to Stephen's arrest.

In chapter 7, Stephen does a passionate speech in his defense when confronting the council at Sanhedrin, which is the Jewish high court. When Stephen is asked if the charges of blasphemy against him are true, he launches into a thorough recounting of Israel's history. He reminds them how God has remained faithful, but they keep rejecting his messengers. Stephen says they reject the holy spirit, just like their stiff neck ancestors. When the council members hear these accusations, they are infuriated and have him killed. They drag him out of the city and begin to stone him. As he dies, Stephen asks the lord to not hold this sin against his killers. Among the witnesses of this event is Saul, who later becomes the apostle Paul.

In chapter 8, a great persecution breaks out against the church in Jerusalem, all the apostles were scattered throughout Judea and Samaria. Godly men buried Stephen and mourned deeply for him. Saul tried to destroy the church by going from house to house, dragging both men and woman to prison. Although the followers were scattered, they use it as an opportunity to preach the gospel to new regions. Starting out with Phillip, who was one of the seven deacons. Phillip preaches in Samaria and performs miracles, bringing joy to the city. Samarians were known to be enemies of the Israelites, but many Samaritans believe and are baptized, including Simon, a man formerly known for sorcery. An angel of the lord directs Philip to the road from Jerusalem to Gaza, where he encounters an Ethiopian eunuch. Philip explains Isaiah's prophecy that the eunuch was reading, leading to the eunuch's baptism and conversion. The eunuch confesses they believe that Jesus Christ is the son of God. Later, the spirit takes Philip away, and he continues to preach the gospel in other towns.

In chapter 9, Saul converts into Paul. His name was still Saul at the time, and Saul was still breathing out murderous threats against the lord's disciples. He was the biggest enemy and persecutor of Jesus' followers. When Saul was on his way to Damascus, a light from heaven suddenly shines down on him and strikes him. It was followed by him hearing a voice from the heavens asking him why he persecutes Jesus. Saul was blinded by the light and could not see for three days, so his companions had to guide him. The lord appears to Ananias, instructing him to lay his hands on Saul to restore his sight. Saul is baptized, eats, and regains his strength. Saul spends time with the disciples in Damascus and immediately starts preaching about Jesus. The disciples were hesitant and fearful because they knew Sauls past. However, Barnabas accepts Saul and introduces him to the apostles. Saul preaches boldly in the name of the Lord. As Peter traveled the country, he went to visit the lord's people who lived in Lydda, and found a man named Aeneas, who was paralyzed. Peter heals the man.

In chapter 10, it is a pivotal moment where the gospel is extended to the gentiles, breaking down the barrier between Jews and non-Jews in the early church. There was a roman centurion man named Cornelius, he experiences a vision where he saw an angel of God, who told him to go to Joppa and find Simon Peter. Cornelius obeys and sends servants and a soldier to find Peter. Peter was praying on the rooftop and while waiting for a meal to be prepared he fell into a trance; he receives a vision. God tells Peter that Jesus has already cleansed everything, it is no longer needed to say animals are clean or unclean to eat, like with Jewish dietary laws. Peter was pondering what the meaning of the vision was, and Cornelius's messengers arrived. Peter, guided by the spirit accompanies them back to Caesarea where Cornelius' house is. Upon arrival, Cornelius explains his vision and why he sent for Peter. Cornelius falls to his knees in reverence or respect, but Peter tells him to stand up saying he is only a man himself. Peter acknowledges that God does not show favoritism and accepts all people from every nation. Peter shares the message of Jesus Christ, his ministry, crucifixion, and resurrection. He declares that everyone who believes in Jesus receives forgiveness of sins. While Peter was still speaking these words, the holy spirit came on to all who heard the message. The believers who were with Peter were astonished that the gift of the holy spirit has been poured out and made available even for gentiles. Peter says they received the holy spirit just as they had, then ordered that they be baptized in the name of Jesus Christ.

In chapter 11, the themes in this section come together with the founding of the first large multiethnic church, which is in Antioch. Those who had been scattered by the persecution that broke out when Stephen was killed traveled as far as Phoenicia, Cyprus and Antioch, spreading the word only among Jews. Some of them from Cyprus and Cyrene, went to Antioch and began to speak to Greeks also, telling them the good news about the Lord Jesus. The lord's hand was with them, and a great number of people believed and turned to the lord. The Antioch church led many gentiles to the lord with the help of Barnabas and Paul. It was the first time the term Christians was used.

In chapter 12, Herod arrested some who belonged to the church, he had James the brother of John, put to death by sword. Peter was also captured, but makes a miraculous escape on the eve of his trial, guided by an angel of the lord who wakes him up and frees him from his chains, leading him out of the prison. Peter goes to Mary's house, where many believers have gathered to pray. Peter is let in and tells them about his miraculous escape, asking them to relay the news to James and the brothers. In the morning, there is a great commotion among the soldiers over Peter's escape. When they fail to find Peter, Herod interrogates and executes the guards. Herod is struck down by an angel of the lord, and he dies. Despite the chaotic events, the word of God continues to spread and grow.

Chapter 13-20 Missionary journeys

In chapter 13 (Asia Minor), It shifts focus from Peter and others to Paul and Barnabas. Paul and Barnabas face opposition and trials, but have persistence in their commitment to proclaim the good news of Jesus. Their courage and faith, guided by the holy spirit, show the heart and spirit of missionary work. Barnabas, Saul, and John Mark sail to Cyprus and proclaim the Word of God in the synagogues first. Paul who is filled with the holy spirit, enters a synagogue and delivers a sermon tracing Israel's history and proclaiming Jesus as the savior. Many Jews and gentiles were following Paul and Barnabas; they encouraged them to continue their work by the grace of God. On the next sabbath, the whole city gathered to hear the word of the lord. When the Jews saw the big crowds, they instantly felt jealous, they started contradicting the things he was saying and abusing him. Paul and Barnabas announce boldly that since the Jews reject the word of God and do not want eternal life; they are speaking to the gentiles now. The lord says he has made a light for the gentiles, so that salvation may reach the ends of the earth. The gentiles rejoice, and the word of the lord spreads throughout the region. The Jewish leaders stirred up persecution against Paul and Barnabas, they expel them from their region. So, they shook the dust off their feet as a warning to them and went to Iconium, and the disciples were filled with joy and with the holy spirit.

In chapter 14 (Asia Minor), at Iconium, Paul and Barnabas went to the Jewish synagogue first as usual. They spoke so effectively that a great number of Jews and Greeks believed. Paul and Barnabas spent considerable time there, speaking boldly for the lord and performing miracles. Some unbelieving Jews stir up gentiles against them, causing division. Some sided with the Jews, others with the apostles. There was a plot among both Jews and gentiles to mistreat and stone them, but they found out about it and fled. They went to the Lycaonian cities of Lystra and Derbe and to the surrounding country, where they continued to preach the gospel. In Lystra, Paul heals a man crippled from birth, which leads the crowd to mistake Paul and Barnabas for Gods. Paul and Barnabas quickly correct the misunderstanding, saying they too are only human like them. They clarify they are here to spread the good news and speak on God's grace. They stoned Paul and dragged him outside the city, thinking he was dead. However, when the disciples gather around him, he gets up and goes back into the city. The next day, he and Barnabas leave for Derbe. Paul and Barnabas continue preaching and make many disciples in Derbe. They then revisit Lystra, Iconium, and Antioch. They strengthen the disciples, encouraging them to remain true to the faith despite persecutions, and they appoint elders in each church. They travel through Pisidia, Pamphylia, Perga, Attalia, and finally return to Antioch in Syria. They gather the church and report all that God had done through them, especially opening the door of faith to the gentiles.

In chapter 15, there is a theological dispute about whether gentiles need to adhere to Jewish law. Paul discovers there are some Jewish Christians in Antioch who claim that when gentiles become Christians, they must adhere to all Jewish laws to be saved. Such as circumcision, kosher food, and obeying the sabbath. If not, then they cannot join the Jesus family. Paul and Barnabas disagree with these statements and take the debate to a leadership council in Jerusalem. During the council, Peter asserts that God has accepted the gentiles and that they should not be burdened with the laws of Moses. God's plan was to create a new covenant that is acceptable for the entire world, not everyone is born ethnically Jewish and do not need to adhere to every Jewish law. James, the leader of the Jerusalem church agrees and suggests writing a letter to the gentiles asking them to abstain from food polluted by idols, from sexual immorality, and from meat of strangled animals. It is his judgment that they should not make it difficult for the gentiles who are turning to God. God did not discriminate between Jews and gentiles, for he purified their hearts by faith. God knows everyone's hearts and accepted them by giving them the holy spirit, just as they are. He says that not even the Jewish people were able to adhere to all the laws, and it is only by the grace of the Lord Jesus that one may be saved. The council agrees with James's proposal and sends Judas and Silas, Barnabas, and Paul to deliver the letter to the gentile believers in Antioch, Syria, and Cilicia. The delivery of the letter brings great joy to the believers. This was a pivotal moment for followers of Jesus because it showed membership is not based off ethnicity or torah observance, membership is based off trusting and obeying Jesus Christ. At the end of the chapter, Paul and Barnabas part ways to preach at separate locations.

In chapter 16, it details Paul's second missionary journey, focusing on his travels with Timothy and Silas through Macedonia. Paul and Silas revisit Derbe and Lystra where they meet Timothy, a young disciple who had a Jewish mother and a Greek father. Paul recruits Timothy to help with ministry among Jewish communities. As they traveled from town to town, they delivered messages and decisions from the apostles and elders in Jerusalem for the people to obey. The churches were strengthened in faith and grew in numbers daily. Paul has a vision to go to Macedonia to help the people over there. They travel to Philippi, a roman colony, where they meet Lydia. After Lydia hears Paul preach, she and her entire household are baptized. Paul and Silas encounter a fortune teller slave girl; Paul casts the demons out of her in Jesus name. The owners of the slave girl are enraged because they were exploiting her for money. They have Paul and Silas publicly beaten and imprisoned. That night, an earthquake shakes the prison which opens all the doors and loosens chains. They share the gospel with the jailer, who ends up giving his life to Jesus along with his household. The city officials say they falsely beat and imprisoned the two men Paul and Silas, so they were released and depart from Philippi.

In chapter 17, it shows Paul's missionary journey through Thessalonica, Berea, and Athens. They encounter various groups of people and preach the good news of Jesus. Paul, Silas, and Timothy arrive in Thessalonica and go to the synagogues first, as they usually do. He reasons with them from the scriptures. He is explaining and proving that Jesus is the messiah, and had to suffer and rise from the dead. Some jealous Jews rounded up some bad characters, formed a mob, and started a riot in the city. Next Paul and Silas went to Berea, they had more of a noble character there, and examined the scriptures and Paul's message closely. Many people there believe in Jesus, including Greek men and woman, but Jews hear about it and stir up trouble by agitating crowds. Paul heads off to Athens while Timothy and Silas stayed in Berea. Paul was disturbed to see how much idolatry was going on in Athens. He runs into some philosophers and has a debate with them. Paul explains that there is a divine creator of the world who will judge and rose from the dead. Some of the philosophers sneered after hearing about resurrection and made sarcastic comments saying, "what is he babbling about?" while others gave their life to Jesus.

In chapter 18, Paul leaves Athens and goes to Corinth. When he arrives, he met a Jew named Aquila. Paul begins preaching full time in the synagogue, testifying to the Jews that Jesus is the messiah. Some Jews reject his message, so he shifts his focus to the gentiles. Crispus the synagogue leader gave his life to Christ, along with his entire household. Many of the Corinthians who heard Paul believed and were baptized. The lord spoke to Paul in a vision telling him to keep on speaking, and to not be silent or afraid of opposition. He told Paul that he would be protected against any harm or attacks. So Paul stayed in Corinth for a year and a half, teaching the word of God. After Paul's long stay in Corinth, he sailed off for Syria accompanied by Priscilla and Aquila. The chapter shows the conversion of gentiles with the help of an Alexandria native named Apollos, who had a thorough knowledge of scriptures and plays an important role in the early church. Paul goes from place to place on missionary journeys, expanding the church beyond its Jewish origins in the face of opposition. Paul went from Ephesus, to Caesarea, to Jerusalem, then to Antioch. After spending some time in Antioch, Paul sets out from there and goes throughout the region of Galatia and Phrygia, strengthening all the disciples.

In chapter 19, Apollos stayed at Corinth, while Paul arrived in Ephesus. Paul entered the synagogue and spoke boldly there for three months, arguing persuasively about the kingdom of God, but some refused to believe. So Paul took the disciples and began doing daily discussions in the lecture hall of Tyrannus, which went on for two years. He explains that they need to be baptized in the name of Jesus to receive the holy spirit. All the Jews and Greeks who lived in the province of Asia heard the word of God. Miracles, healings, and exorcisms by Paul went on during this time. Some Jews tried to do exorcisms themselves in the name of Jesus and Paul, the demon possessed man was like "I know Jesus and Paul, but who are you?" The man who had the evil spirit jumped them, giving them such a beating that they ran out of the house bleeding and naked. When this became known to the Jews and Greeks living in Ephesus, they were all seized with fear, and the name of the Jesus was held in high honor. A number of them who had practiced sorcery brought their old magic books and scrolls, then burned them publicly. The chapter ends with a silversmith named Demetrius, who made shrines of Greek Gods. He was furious because he said Paul's preaching would hurt his business, so he incites a riot. He got other silversmiths and workers in similar trades to form a mob. The city clerk quieted the crowd by telling them that these men have not robbed or done any serious crime, and if they have a problem with their teaching then they need to take it up in court legally. The clerk said that the courts are open, and they can press charges if they want, dismissing the assembly.

In chapter 20, it is Paul's final missionary journey through Greece and Asia minor as he goes back to Jerusalem. He finds out some Jews are plotting to kill him as he was preparing to go to Syria, so instead decided to go back through Macedonia. Paul spends a week in Troas, where he puts his arms around a young man named Eutychus, raising him from the dead. Paul travels south on boat and meets with Ephesian elders, delivering a powerful farewell speech. He testifies of the good news of God's grace, he warns them to have discernment against false teachers, and also to be shepherds of the church of God. When Paul finished speaking, he knelt down with all of them and prayed. They all wept as they embraced him and kissed him.

In chapter 21, Paul heads off to Jerusalem despite the warnings not to go there because of the danger. He sailed from Miletus to Tyre, then to Caesarea where he stayed with Phillip the evangelist. Paul arrives in Jerusalem to meet with James and the elders; he reports in detail what God has done among the gentiles through his ministry. When they heard this they praised God, but brought up their concerns about Jews obsessing over the laws of Moses. Some of the Jews are talking, saying that Paul is telling people to abandon the laws of Moses. To address these concerns, the elders suggest for Paul to do a purification ritual to demonstrate his adherence to Jewish law. So Paul goes to the temple and Jews from the province of Asia saw him there, they stirred up a whole crowd to start a riot. They shouted at Paul saying that this is the man telling everyone everywhere against their people and laws. The whole city was fired up and came running from all directions. The crowd seized Paul, dragged him from the temple, and attempted to kill him. While they were trying to kill him, the news that Jerusalem was in an uproar reached the Roman commander. The commander arrested and bound Paul with two chains. The violence of the mob was so great that he had to be carried by the soldiers. The crowd kept shouting to get rid of him.

In chapter 22, Paul speaks his defense to the crowd as the soldiers were about to take him to barracks. He starts speaking in Aramaic, which gains the crowds attention and silences them. Paul identifies himself as a Jew who is thoroughly trained in the laws of their ancestors, and explains how he was persecuting followers of Jesus because he thought the same as them before. He brings up his road to Damascus where he was suddenly blinded by a bright light from heaven. He describes how he was healed and was instructed to preach the gospel to the world. Paul says he was called to be a witness to all people of the things he has seen and heard. He says that God revealed to him a mission to preach to the gentiles, which angers the crowd. They were listening to him before this statement, but they will not accept that God wants salvation for both Jew and gentile. The crowd started raising their voices, shouting for Paul to be removed from earth and saying that he is not fit to live. The commander ordered for him to be taken away. Paul asked them if it was legal for them to take away a Roman citizen who had not been found guilty. The commander was alarmed when he realized that he had put Paul, a Roman citizen in chains. So the next day he released Paul to the Jewish council to stand before them.

In chapter 23, it describes Paul's appearance before the Jewish council Sanhedrin. Paul looked straight at them and said, "My brothers I have fulfilled my duty to God in all good conscience to this day." Paul spoke his case which led to a divided council, it got so heated that the pharisees and sadducees were yelling at each other vigorously saying Paul did nothing wrong. The dispute became so violent that the Roman commander thought Paul was going to be torn to pieces. The commander ordered for troops to take Paul away from them and bring him into the barracks, which is like a military base for Romans. A group of forty or more Jews plotted to kill Paul, they made an oath to not eat or drink until he was dead. The son of Paul's sister heard of this plot and went to the barracks to warn him. The forty Jews were going to ambush Paul at his next meeting at Sanhedrin, so the Romans take action to protect Paul. They sent Paul to Caesarea under heavy protection because of the danger he was in, along with a letter explaining the situation. Paul arrives to Governor Felix, who says he will hear out the case once his accusers get there. Paul was kept under guard at Herod's place.

In chapter 24, it details Paul's trial before Governor Felix in Caesarea. Some of the Jewish leaders went down to Caesarea to bring their case and charges against Paul before the governor. They accuse Paul of being a troublemaker who stirred up riots among the Jews. They said he was the ringleader of a cult and accused him of desecrating the temple. They said Lysias took Paul away with great violence out of their hands. The other Jews jumped in to confirm these accusations were true. Paul refutes these accusations and says he was only in Jerusalem for a short time and that his accusers did not find him arguing with anyone at the temple or stirring up any crowds. Paul says they cannot prove these things, and that he was only practicing his faith according to the prophets of their ancestors and of God. Paul states it concerns the resurrection of the dead that he stands trial on that day, they have nothing on him otherwise they would have found him guilty prior at Sanhedrin. Then Felix dismissed them and adjourned the proceedings. Felix is aware of Paul's innocence but is delaying judgement and puts him on house arrest. He is delaying judgement because he hopes to get bribe money from Paul or his followers. Two years pass by with no judgment on Paul's case and eventually Felix is succeeded by a new governor named Porcius Festus.

In chapter 25, Governor Festus faces pressure from the chief priests and Jewish leaders, who urge him to send Paul to Jerusalem for trial, intending to ambush and assassinate him along the way. Festus refuses and said he will hold Paul's trial in Caesarea, and if they want to bring any charges they can do it there. So the Jewish leaders go to Paul's trial and bring many serious charges against him, but they could not prove anything. Paul makes his defense by saying he has done nothing wrong against Jewish law or the temple, or against Caesar. Festus wanted to please the Jews and do them a favor, so he asks Paul if he is willing to stand trial in Jerusalem. Paul knows the Jewish leaders intentions, so he invokes his rights as a Roman citizen, and appeals to Caesar. Festus discussed it with his council, and agreed to send Paul to Rome to be judged by Caesar. The chapter ends with king Agrippa arriving at Caesarea. Festus discusses Paul's case with the king, which interests him in wanting to hear Paul speak himself, setting up the scene before his trial.

In chapter 26, it starts out with Paul standing trial, king Agrippa tells him he has permission to speak. Paul politely acknowledged the king and said how fortunate he is to stand before him in defense against all the accusations from the Jews. Paul details his past as a persecutor, he said he did everything possible to oppose all who followed Jesus of Nazareth. He said he was so obsessed with persecuting them, that he even went to foreign cities to hunt them down. He explains his miraculous conversion on the road to Damascus, where he encountered Jesus and was appointed as a servant and witness of what he had seen. Paul says he is just following the vision from heaven, preaching to the gentiles about repentance. He says he is just quoting scripture from the prophets who said the messiah will suffer, rise from the dead, and bring light to his own people and to the gentiles. Festus thinks Paul is mad, but king Agrippa was more familiar with Jewish customs, so he was more interested in Paul's words. Festus, Agrippa, and Bernice all agree Paul has done nothing worthy of death or imprisonment. Agrippa mentioned that Paul could have been set free right there if he had not appealed to Caesar. An appeal to Caesar cannot be taken back because the act is final and legally binding to the supreme roman court. So Paul will be going to Rome.

In chapter 27, Paul is leaving Caesarea and sets sail to Rome, Italy. Paul and the other prisoners were handed over to a centurion named Julius. On their way, they face violent storms and winds so bad that they had to throw cargo overboard, and they lost control of the ship. This led to the destruction of the boat, and the sailors gave up all hope of survival. Paul becomes the source of hope and guidance because he received a vision from God. The vision said that neither him nor the two hundred seventy-six passengers would die. He assures the crew of their safety and feeds them. Paul ordered those who could swim to jump first and get to land. The rest were told to get there on planks, or to use a piece of the ship to float on. In this way everyone reached land safely.

In chapter 28, once safely on shore, they find out that the island was called Malta. The locals on the island show kindness to them. Paul gets bit by a venomous snake, and it has no effect, which amazes the island locals. Paul demonstrates God's power by healing the chief official of the island, as well as healing others. The people on the island were appreciative in many ways and honored them, they even furnished them with supplies when they were ready to sail. After three months, they set sail and arrive in Rome where believers greet Paul. He is put under house arrest and allowed to live by himself with a soldier to guard him. For two years Paul stayed there in his own rented house and welcomed all who came to see him. He proclaimed the kingdom of God and taught about the Lord Jesus Christ, with boldness and without hindrance.

Romans

In Romans, Paul addresses the believers in Rome. This is his longest letter ever written for missionary purposes. To the Jesus followers living directly under Caesar, he is appealing to bring the gospel to the western part of the empire. God's divine plan has been revealed through the prophets up until the messiah Jesus. The message shows that God has always been faithful to his covenant with Israel. The letter shows that even Jewish law could not defeat sin, it can only be done through God's grace. God has come to rescue the Jews and gentiles through the death and resurrection of Jesus. The offer of life through Jesus remains for all, in the end God's mercy will triumph over judgment. Baptism into Jesus breaks the power of evil and the holy spirit leads people into a new life. God welcomes salvation to all of creation.

In chapter 1, Paul starts off by referring to himself as a servant for the Lord Jesus, saying he is called upon to be an apostle and spread the gospel of God. He acknowledges Jesus as the descendant of David, and the through the spirit he was appointed son of God. In the letters, Paul sends greetings to all in Rome who are loved by God and called to be saints. He calls on all the holy people of Rome and gentiles, wishing grace and peace be among them from God the Father and from the Lord Jesus Christ. Paul talks about the power of the gospel, and he is obligated to all people, including both Greeks and non-Greeks, also both wise and foolish. Paul says he is eager to preach the word to them. He says he is not ashamed of the gospel because it reveals the power of God that brings salvation to everyone who believes, first to the Jew, then to the gentile. He says the righteousness of God is revealed in the gospel and says, "The righteous will live by faith."

The wrath of God is being revealed from heaven against all the godlessness and wickedness of people, who suppress the truth by their wickedness. All nations on earth have been trapped in the cycle of sin and are unable to break free from sin on their own. Since the creation of the world, God says he has revealed his invisible qualities through his eternal power and divine nature. God has made himself clearly seen, so that people are without excuse. They turn away from God and welcomed idolatry. They exchanged the truth about God for a lie, and worshiped created things rather than the creator. They pledge their loyalties in things that are not from God. They never glorified God, nor gave thanks to him. Their thinking became futile, and their foolish hearts were darkened. They claimed to be wise, but they had become fools. Therefore, God gave them over to their desires, he gave people the free will to choose their sinful desires within their hearts. God gave them over to their shameful lusts. Their women exchanged natural sexual relations for unnatural ones. They degraded their bodies with one another in impure ways. They sexualized everything and were inflamed with lust for one another. Men committed shameful acts with other men. They did not think it worthwhile to retain the knowledge of God. They have become filled with every kind of wickedness, evil, greed, and corruption. They are full of envy, murders, deceit, and hatred. They gossip and are argumentative. They have become slanderers, God-haters, arrogant, boastful, and rude. They invent new ways of doing evil and disobeying their parents daily. They have no understanding, no loyalty, no love, and no mercy. All humans are guilty of sin, awaiting judgement from God.

In chapter 2, it explains that God is the ultimate just judge who holds everyone accountable for their actions, both Jew and gentile. Paul explains that God is impartial, and judges based off the truth in a person's heart and what they have done. To those who do good, seek glory, and are honorable will have eternal life. But for those who are self-seeking, reject truth, and follow evil, there will be wrath and anger. Paul acknowledges the Jews and the law, emphasizing that those relying on the law alone is not sufficient. God's judgment is based off inward transformation. People challenge others on righteousness and judge others but fail to live up to God's standards themselves. The Jews have misguided confidence in themselves because they recognize the laws and circumcision. Paul tells the Jews that true circumcision is a matter of the heart, performed by the spirit, not by the written code. On the outside one can be a Jew, but inwardly their hearts may be far from God.

In chapter 3, Paul declares that all are guilty of sin, both Jews and gentiles, using quotations from the old testament to support his claims. Therefore, no one will be declared righteous in God's sight. Paul concludes that the law makes us conscious of our sin, and there is a universal sin problem that needs to be judged and paid for. Paul proclaims that the righteousness of God has been made known apart from the law. This righteousness is given through faith in Jesus Christ to all who believe. There is no difference between Jew and gentile, for all have sinned and fall short of the glory of God. Jesus paid the price for the sins of the world when he was presented as a sacrifice of atonement, demonstrating his justice and righteousness. There were unpunished sins committed beforehand that were unresolved. Jesus came as a representative to take in himself all the consequences of sin, pain, and death that humans deserved. He overcame it with his resurrection on the cross. Through his sacrifice and resurrection, new life is made available to all. Paul writes that God justifies those who trust and have faith in Jesus. We are given a new status before God because of what Jesus did on our behalf. Instead of being declared guilty, we are put in a position of being forgiven. Whoever trusts in Jesus will be placed among God's covenant people. God's grace allows people a new future. It is a gift from God for whoever puts their faith in the lord.

In chapter 4, It explores what it takes to be part of God's covenant family. Abraham is used as an example, he was declared righteous by God because of his faith. He also quotes David, who was credited as righteous because of his strong faith in God, apart from works. The declaration of righteousness from God is a gift. For example, the wage from a job is an obligation, not a gift. If one does not work but trusts God, their faith is credited as righteousness. The chapter details Abraham's story, he was promised that he would be a father to many nations. He believed in his heart the promises God made. The promise was delivered because he remained strong in faith. Despite his body being as good as dead because he was approaching old age, he remained true when God told him he would father many nations. He did not waver through unbelief regarding the promise of God but was strengthened in his faith and gave glory to God, being fully persuaded that God had power to do what he had promised. This is what God meant when saying he was credited in righteousness, but these words are not meant for Abraham alone. God will also credit righteousness to those who believe in him, who raised Jesus from the dead. He was delivered over to death for human sins and was raised to life for human justification. Abraham's faith was credited as righteous before his circumcision, proving that righteousness is not tied to the law or circumcision but to faith.

In chapter 5, Paul starts by highlighting that justification through faith gives them peace with God through the Lord Jesus Christ. He says not to dwell in suffering but rejoice, because suffering produces perseverance. Suffering produces endurance, character, and hope. Paul shows the depth of God's love which is manifested through Christ's death. He assures that people are reconciled to God through the death of his son and saved through his life. Sin and death entered the world through one man Adam, and that sin and death came to all people because of that. Humanity has become slave to sin, and the wages of sin is death. It compares Adam's sin with death and Christ's gift with life. Although one man's disobedience made many sinners, the life of Jesus make many righteous. Sin reigned in death, so that grace might reign through righteousness to bring eternal life through Jesus Christ.

    In chapter 6, it explains that believers are dead to sin, and alive in Christ where they are no longer slaves to sin. Paul reminds the followers of Jesus in Rome that following Christ is entering a new life. Their old selves are crucified with Christ to destroy the power of sin. Through their baptism, their new selves are raised just like Christ. So, when someone follows Jesus, their life becomes joined to his and given new life. What is true in Christ is now true in them. They are liberated to fully love God and other humans. Paul urges believers to regard themselves as dead to sin but alive to God in Christ Jesus. Paul explores the believer's relationship with sin and the transformative power of God's grace.

    In chapter 7, it explains that the law does not save, it just revealed the sinful nature of humans. They were struggling to understand the relationship between sin and flesh. They ask what the purpose of the laws and commands were if someone can just be redeemed of sin. Paul says the commands of the torah were good and showed God's will on how to live, but every law was broken. They rebelled just like Adam, and it was not enough to fix their sinful hearts and human desires. Giving specific moral laws to follow did not fix the problem of sinful hearts. These rules made Israel even more guilty if anything since they should have known better. Paul summarizes that the enemy and evil have prevailed over the human heart. A savior is needed because a list of rules was not enough. Paul shows the role of the law in amplifying the sinful nature. He discusses the complexities of human nature, explaining how the law, while good and holy, reveals their sinful tendencies, showing humans desperately need deliverance through Christ. It calls us to lean into the grace offered through Jesus Christ. Paul says that if he does what he does not want to do, it is no longer him who does it, but it is sin living in him that does it. He finds this law at work, although he wants to do good, evil is right there with him. His inner being delights in God's law, but he sees another law of sin at work in him, waging war against his mind, making him a prisoner of the law of sin at work within him. He says he is a wretched man and asks who will save him from this body that is subject to death. He answers his question by thanking God, who delivers him through Jesus Christ. That he himself in his mind is a slave to God's law, but in his sinful nature is a slave to the law of sin.

    In chapter 8, it talks about life through the spirit. Paul assures believers through Jesus Christ, the law of the spirit who gives life has set them free from the law of sin and death. God sent his own son in the likeness of sinful flesh to be a sin offering. Jesus paid for and dealt with all the sin through his death and resurrection. The spirit has been released to the new covenant family so that their hearts may be transformed, so they can truly love God and their neighbors. Paul explains the contrast between living according to the flesh and the spirit. He says those controlled by the spirit have life, peace, and live according to the spirits desires. Those who live according to the flesh have their minds set on what the flesh desires, they are hostile towards God and cannot please him. Paul says the ones who are led by the spirit belong to Christ. The spirit that raised Jesus from the dead is living in them. He who raised Christ will also give life to their mortal bodies because the spirit resides in them. Paul comforts believers by stating that their present sufferings are not worth comparing with the glory that will be revealed in them. The creation waits in eager expectation for the children of God to be revealed. The spirit will help them in their weaknesses and intercede in their struggles. God brings salvation to anyone who seeks. Paul concludes with a message of God's endless love; nothing can separate them from the love of God that is in Lord Jesus.

In chapter 9, Paul is in anguish over Israel and expresses deep sorrow for his fellow Israelites because they have not recognized Jesus as the Messiah. God is sovereign and makes predestined choices based on one's heart or their character. For example, God already made the choice and promise that Sarah will bore a son named Isaac, whose offspring will be as numerous as the stars in the sky. Although he was not the first born, God's choice in Isaac was already appointed. Another example is through Jacob and Esau, where God already declared that the older will serve the younger before the twins were even born. This shows the sovereignty of God, and his choices are not always based off birthright. Paul shows how God always chose a subset of Abraham's descendants to carry out the covenant promises. God promises a new covenant family that extends to all families that have Jesus in their hearts, not just descendants of Jewish people. Humans have rejected God's will since long ago. Scripture says God raised pharaoh up for the very purpose of displaying God's power and name to all the earth. Humans rejection of God and hardened hearts allowed him to accomplish his redemptive plan. Paul quotes the prophets Hosea and Isaiah to highlight the inclusion of gentiles and the remnant of Israel in God's salvation plan.

In chapter 10, Paul says Israel, who pursued the law of righteousness, did not succeed because they pursued it through works and not by faith. It explains that salvation comes through faith in Jesus and not adhering to the laws of Moses. Many Jews were zealous for God but lacked the true knowledge of God's righteousness found in Jesus. Jesus is the fulfilment and the end of the law. The message concerning salvation is this, if someone declares with their mouth aloud that Jesus is lord, and truly believes in their heart that God raised him from the dead, then they will be saved. For it is with the heart that someone believes and is justified, and it is with the mouth they professes faith and are saved. Anyone who believes in him will never be put to shame. There is no difference between Jew or gentile, the same lord is lord and richly blesses all who call on him. Everyone who calls on the name of the lord will be saved.

In chapter 11, The Jewish people are struggling to understand because they are basing their judgement on how well they are following the torah. They are unable to see what God has done for humanity and the new covenant he created for the world based off faith. Paul writes about the future of Israel. He begins by asserting that God has not rejected or written off his people, naming his own Israelite lineage as evidence. He mentions the time of Elijah when God had preserved a remnant of seven thousand who had not bowed to Baal and similarly, at the present time, there is a remnant chosen by grace. He uses an analogy of an olive tree to depict how gentiles are attached into the developed olive tree that was just Israel before. He cautioned them against arrogance and emphasizing their dependence on the root. He says all the branches are neutral and none are superior to another. Salvation is attainable to all who want to join the tree, which made some jews jealous. It states that after the full number of gentiles has come in, then all Israel will be saved. Despite their disobedience, God's mercy is still available for all. Paul writes about the depth of the riches of the wisdom and knowledge of God; all things are from him, through him, and for him and glory be to him.

In chapter 12, it provides an outline for Christian living within one's self and community. It calls for them to offer their bodies as a living sacrifice to please God in light of his mercy. Paul urges people not to conform to this world, and to become transformed through the renewing of the mind. It says that the believers make up the body of Christ, and although they form one body, each member belongs to all the others. Each member of the body of Christ can have different functions or gifts. Some have the gift to prophesy, some to serve, some to teach, some to lead, and others to give encouragement. Each gift should be used cheerfully within the body of Christ to benefit the whole community. The chapter lists how believers are called to love one another within life and relationships. Paul writes about sincere love; he says to "hate what is evil and cling to what is good. Be devoted to one another in love, honor one another above yourselves. Be joyful in hope, patient in affliction, faithful in prayer. Practice hospitality and bless those who persecute you. Do not be conceited or proud thinking your above other people, be willing to associate with people of low position. Live in harmony with one another. Do not repay anyone evil for evil. Do not take revenge, trust that the lord is the one who will judge. If your enemy is hungry or thirsty, give them food and water. Offer kindness instead of acting with revenge. Do not be overcome by evil, but overcome evil with good."

In chapter 13, it starts out with encouraging believers to follow the laws of their governments, pay their taxes, and honor those who are in public service. This is not blind submission, but rather a general respect for order. The next section explains that love fulfills the law because loving others is the ultimate expression of someone's faith. Then it ends by urging believers to wake up from their slumber because salvation is near. It says to clothe themselves with Jesus Christ, and to not think about how to gratify the desires of the flesh.

In chapter 14, it is about how followers of Jesus should interact with each other. Paul says to accept other people even if their faith is weak, without fighting over matters. The chapter emphasizes unity and love within communities despite any disagreements. It urges them to avoid judging, instead build each other up and be accepting. Everyone will have to stand before God's judgment, so who is anyone to judge a brother or sister. He says if someone has a different conviction on whether food is clean or not and they become distressed, then that person is not acting in love anymore. It says to make every effort to do what leads to peace, and to not destroy the work of God over food. For the kingdom of God is not about judging what a person consumes, it is about righteousness, peace, and joy in the holy spirit. So whatever someone believes about certain things should be kept between themselves and God.

In chapter 15, it says to build up and do good to their neighbors. Paul wishes for God, who gives endurance and encouragement, to give them the same attitude of mind toward each other that Jesus had, so that one mind and one voice may glorify God the Father and the Lord Jesus Christ. He says to accept one another, just as Christ accepted them, in order to praise God. Paul explains that Christ became a servant to the Jews on behalf of God's truth, so that the divine promises may be confirmed, and for God to be glorified for his mercy. Paul quotes old testament scripture confirming the gentiles role was always included in God's plan for salvation. Paul's ministry is a call from God to bring Christ to the gentiles and explains this is the reason for his boldness in writing. He shares that he has proclaimed the Gospel of Christ, from Jerusalem all the way to Illyricum, and aims to preach it everywhere Christ is not known. The chapter ends with Paul's plan to visit Rome on his way to Spain.

In chapter 16, Paul finishes the book by sending his greetings, warnings, blessings, and final prayers. Paul gives a shoutout and acknowledgement to all the early church leaders who put their life on the line to spread the word of God. Paul commends a women named Phoebe, who he calls their sister and a deacon of the church in Cenchreae. She had the honor of delivering this letter to the Romans. Paul lists other individuals including Priscilla and Aquila, his fellow workers in Christ who risked their lives for him. He says the churches of gentiles and himself are grateful to them. He mentions Epenetus, who was the first convert to Christ in the province of Asia. There is Mary, who worked very hard for them. Also there is Greet Andronicus and Junia, who were his fellow prisoners that were with Christ before him. Paul proceeds to greet and acknowledge a list of names who are in the lord and helped spread the good news.

      Paul warns to watch out for those who cause divisions and speak of things that are contrary to the word of God in scripture. These people are not serving the lord, they are only serving their own appetite and self-desires. These false teachers deceive the minds of naive people through their smooth talk and flattery. Paul says that he rejoices and commends peoples obedience, but urges them to be wise about what is good or evil. Then he assures them that God will soon crush Satan under their feet, the grace of the lord will be with them. Paul concludes with a declaration of glory and praise to God. The mystery of prophetic writings has been revealed and made known by the command of the eternal God. The revelation has been hidden for ages, but now God has established them in accordance with his gospel, so that all the gentiles might come to obedience through faith; to the only wise God be glory forever through Jesus Christ. He wishes grace of the Lord Jesus Christ with them all.

1 Corinthians

In the previous books Paul went to Macedonia, which is northern Grece, then fled to Achaia, which is southern Greece. He visited the city of Corinth, which was a wealthy commercial center that served as a marketplace for trade. Many people there became believers, so he stayed there for a year and a half to teach them. Paul got report that the church in Corinth was having problems, and this is his first letter to the them. This letter is directed towards them but has a timeless message of love and unity.

In chapter 1, the letter starts out acknowledging the church of God in Corinth, and says to those sanctified in Christ Jesus and called to be his holy people, together with all those everywhere who call on the name of our Lord Jesus Christ. Grace and peace to them from God the Father and the Lord Jesus Christ. Paul calls for unity within the church. He acknowledges the disagreements within the church, some identifying with different leaders such as Paul, Apollos, or Cephas. They grouped up with their favorite leaders and talked badly about the others. Paul emphasizes that it was Christ who was crucified for them, and that the focus should be on Christ and his message, not on who baptizes them. Paul highlights God's wisdom and power, showing in contrast to human wisdom. He explains that the message of the cross is perceived as foolishness to the intellects who will eventually perish. The power of God is in those who are saved. God will destroy the wisdom of the wise, and the intelligence of the intelligent will get frustrated. He asks who is this wise person, the philosopher of an age, or the wisdom seeking Greeks, or the teachers of law. God chose the foolish things of the world to shame the wise and strong, so that no one may boast in his presence. God's wisdom is beyond human wisdom and through Jesus, wisdom is given from God to find righteousness, holiness, and redemption.

In chapter 2, it continues on the same topic of God's wisdom. Paul's says his testimony about God is not from human wisdom, it is a demonstration of God's power and the spirits power. God's wisdom is revealed by the spirit, which was hidden and predestined for glory before time began, a wisdom that none of the rulers of that age understood. This wisdom is revealed through the spirit, for the spirit searches all things, even the deep things of God. Paul describes the difference between a person with or without the spirit and gives an example. The example is that only a person's self or spirit knows their own thoughts within them. In the same way no one knows the thoughts of God except the spirit of God. What they have received is not the spirit of the world, but the spirit who is from God, so that they may understand what God has freely given. The person without the spirit does not accept the things that come from the spirit of God and considers them foolishness, they cannot understand them because they are discerned only through the spirit. The person with the spirit discerns all things with the mind of Christ.

In chapter 3, Paul compares them to infants in Christ that still need to be fed milk and not solid food yet. He points out their worldly behavior like jealousy and arguing, which caused divisions among them. It should be centered around Jesus and love, not a popularity contest about which church is best. Paul emphasizes that church leaders are still servants to God, each serving the role God assigned to them. While one plants and another waters, it is God who gives the growth. The one who plants and the one who waters have one purpose, and they will each be rewarded according to their own labor. Paul refers to a building as a metaphor, with Jesus as the foundation, and others are building on it. He says to imagine themselves as coworkers and it is God's building, his service, and his field. He says they themselves are God's temple, and God's spirit dwells amongst their midst. He warns every builder to be careful how they build because the quality of their work will be judged on judgment day. The builder's work that survives will receive a reward, while the ones whose work does not survive will suffer loss, but will still be saved. The wisdom of this world is foolishness in God's sight. The lord knows the thoughts of the wise are futile. He warns them not to deceive themselves, and not to value worldly wisdom over God's wisdom. All things of them is Christ, and Christ is of God.

In chapter 4, Paul shows the nature of true apostleship, and being a servant of the lord. He explains that human judgement, including self-judgement, is inconsequential compared to the lord's judgement. God will bring to light what is hidden in darkness and will reveal the motives of hearts. Paul says his conscious is clear, but it does not make him innocent because it is the lord who judges. Paul writes about the apostles suffering for Christ. They are sentenced to death and put to shame for the sake of being a fool for Christ, like a spectacle in front of the world. They suffer hunger, thirst, brutally treated, in rags, and homelessness while laboring with their own hands. Yet they bless those who persecute them and endure it. They become like the scum of the world and when slandered, yet they answer kindly. Paul has an appeal as a father figure and gives a warning. He is like a father because he gave the world writings through the Lord Jesus. He writes these things not to shame them, but to warn them as his dear children. Paul sends Timothy, his son to carry on his work and remind the churches of his ways of life through the Lord Jesus. He warns those who are arrogant that the kingdom of God is not a matter of talk but of power.

In chapter 5, Paul addresses issues related to sexual immorality and calls for moral integrity. He mentions a reported case regarding a man sleeping with his father's wife. The church and community do not remove this guilty person, and Paul asks if they are proud of this. Paul, who is present in spirt passes judgement and instructs the church to deliver the man to Satan for the destruction of the flesh, so his spirit may be saved on the day of the lord. Paul says the boasting is not good and brings up Passover as an example. He encourages the believers to celebrate the feast not with old leaven of malice and wickedness, but with the unleavened bread of sincerity and truth. He warns them to stay away and not to eat with the sexually immoral, the thieves, the drunkards, the idolaters, the adulterers, the greedy, the slanderers, and the swindlers.

In chapter 6, serves as a guideline for dealing with disputes wisely, living morally, and honoring God. It mentions lawsuits among believers. Paul says they are having disputes with one another and taking it up to be judged by ungodly people instead of the lord's people. He reminds them that the lord's people will judge the world, so they are competent and capable of judging trivial cases themselves. He says the very fact that they have lawsuits among them means they have been completely defeated already. There should be no cheating and doing wrong among brothers and sisters of Christ, then reminds them greedy swindlers will not inherit the kingdom of God. It says that the body is a temple and to avoid sexual immorality. Whoever is united with the lord is united with him in spirit. So, if the body is a member of Christ himself, then the body and should not unite with a prostitute. It is written in Genesis that two spirits become one flesh. Flee from sexual immorality. All other sins a person commits are outside the body, but whoever sins sexually, sins against their own body. The body is a temple of the holy spirit and humanity was bought at a price, therefore honor God with the body.

In chapter 7, Paul discusses issues regarding married and unmarried life. He says it is good for a man and woman not to have sexual relations unless married. Each man should have sexual relations with his own wife, and each woman with her own husband. Both wife and husband shall fulfill marital duties to one another. Both wife and husband shall yield authority of their body to one another by mutual consent. He encourages partners not to deprive one another of needs unless both parties agree to a period of time for spiritual reasons and prayer. It addresses issues concerning change of status. God has different roles for different people. Each person should live as a believer in whatever situation the lord has assigned to them, just as God has called them. Keeping God's commands is what counts. Paul advises against separation and divorce among believers, but if it does happen, then they should remain unmarried or be reconciled. If one spouse is a believer and the other is not, that is not grounds for a divorce, stay with them. The kids will be holy through the believing parent. If the unbeliever leaves, let it be so. God has called them to live in peace.

For the unmarried and widows, it is good for them to stay unmarried as Paul does. But if they cannot exercise self-control then they should marry, for it is better to marry than to burn with passion. Also, if a partner in marriage dies, then they are able to remarry. Paul suggests that it is better to stay unmarried just as he is, because marriage will bring about many troubles in this life and he wants to spare them from this. Time is so short and the things of this world in its present form will perish. A person's concerns and thoughts should center around how to grow in relationship with God, not about worldly affairs. Those who have wives should live as if they do not, what he means by that is unmarried men have more time to focus on the lord's interests and how to please him. The married couple are more likely to be attached to things of this world. Regardless, it is not a sin either way whether one chooses to marry or not. Paul is not saying these things to restrict, he is saying it for peoples own good so that they may know how things are. Ultimately, undivided devotion to the lord is the most important.

In chapter 8, Paul writes about foods and when not to eat. He writes about what to do when meat is being sacrificed in the name of other Gods or idols, such as Greek and Roman Gods. Both Jews and gentiles would debate this and Paul states that their first allegiance should be to Jesus. As long as the person killing the animal understands that followers of Jesus believe in a monotheistic God that created all things. As long as there is no misunderstanding and they understand that followers of Jesus cannot worship Jesus and other Gods at the same time, then it is okay to eat whatever is being offered. He says that food does not bring them near to God; they are no worse if they do not eat, and no better if they do. Paul cautions them to not to let their freedoms with food cause a brother or sister to fall into sin. If someone with a weak conscience sees them eating at an idols temple and falls into sin, then that person has sinned for leading a brother or sister astray.

In chapter 9, Paul discusses the rights of an apostle. He says that apostles, and by extension church leaders, have a right to be supported by their congregations, both financially and in other aspects. He is calling on the Corinthians to set aside a right that is theirs. Just as a farmer or soldier benefits from their labor. Despite having these rights, Paul explains that he has not used them. He voluntarily surrenders them because he would rather die than allow anyone to deprive him of his grounds for boasting, and preaching the gospel free of charge. He refers to mosaic law, which says those who serve in the temple get their food from the temple. In the same way, the lord has commanded that those who preach the gospel should receive their living from the gospel. Paul also reminds them of the need for discipline. He compares it to an athlete training for a race that competes for a first-place prize. The imperishable prize from God is far more valuable than any earthly prize, encouraging them to prioritize their bodies and minds.

In chapter 10, it is a reminder of Israels history, it serves as a reminder of the consequences of disobedience and the rewards of faithfulness. Paul reminds the Corinthians that their Israelite ancestors were under the cloud, passed through the sea, and were baptized into Moses. The cloud is a representation of God's presence that accompanied them during their journey from Egypt to the promised land. They all ate the same spiritual food and drink, and drank from the spiritual rock that accompanied them, and that rock was Christ. Nevertheless, God was not pleased with most of them; their bodies were scattered in the wilderness. These things occurred as examples to keep them from setting their hearts on evil things like the Israelites did. He assures them that God is faithful and will not let them be tempted beyond what they can bear. When a person is tempted, God will provide a way out so that they can endure it. Paul references the lord's supper and warns to flee from idolatry. He says a person cannot drink from the cup of the lord and the cup of demons too. They cannot have a part in both the lord's table and the table of demons. It will only provoke the lord. He encourages the Corinthians to seek the good of others before seeking their own good. Everything someone does should be for the glory of God. The earth is the lord's, and everything in it. Paul seeks the good of many, so that they may be saved.

In chapter 11, Paul starts out by talking about the importance of respectability and decency when praying in the church. He says to follow his example, as he follows Christ. He discusses the concept of covering the head in worship and the distinctions between men and women. Paul wants them to realize the head of every man is Christ because man was made in God's image, and the head of a woman is a man, and the head of Christ is God. It emphasizes the order of creation, with woman coming from man. In the lord, woman is not independent of man, nor is man independent of woman. For as woman came from man, man is born from a woman, but everything comes from God. Ultimately the passage represents honor, respect, and authority within the body of Christ. In the next part, the lord's supper was being abused. Paul criticizes the Corinthians for their misconduct during communal meals, which are supposed to be a time of sharing and unity. They have turned it into a time of division. He said their meetings are doing more harm than good. Paul reminds them of the night Jesus was betrayed and broke bread with the disciples. Jesus said the bread was his body and to eat in remembrance of him, and to drink from the cup of his blood representing the new covenant, to drink it in remembrance of him. Paul is reminding them whenever they eat this bread and drink this cup, it is a proclamation of the lord's death until he comes. So then, whoever eats the bread or drinks the cup of the lord in an unworthy manner will be guilty of sinning against the body and blood of the lord. Paul urges everyone to self-reflect and examine themselves first before they eat the bread and drink from the cup. He says the more honest and discerning they are with themselves, the less they will be judged.

In chapter 12, Paul writes about spiritual gifts and their diversity. Also, about unity and diversity within the body of Christ. It emphasizes the importance of every individual believer and their unique contributions to the spirit of God. They are reminded that they all have a place and a purpose within the body of Christ. He says that the variety of spiritual gifts come from the same spirit. There are different kinds of working, but in all of them and in everyone, it is the same God at work. Some examples include wisdom, knowledge, faith, prophecy, miracles, distinguishing between spirits, speaking and interpreting tongues. Each one the manifestations of the spirit is given for the common good. The next part is about the body of Christ and the church. All the believers make up one body, and although though one, has many parts, but all its many parts forms one body, so it is with Christ. He emphasizes the idea that every part, regardless of its role, is crucial for the body to function. The body is made up of many parts that have individual roles, the eye cannot say to the hand I do not need you, and the head cannot say to the feet I do not need you. If the whole body were an eye, where would the sense of hearing be? If the whole body were an ear, where would the sense of smell be? God has placed the parts in the body, every one of them, just as he wanted them to be. There should be no division in the body, its parts should have equal concern for each other. If one part suffers, every part suffers with it. If one part is honored, every part rejoices with it. Paul says they are the body of Christ, and each one of them is a part of it.

In chapter 13, it talks about how love is indispensable and important. Paul highlights the characteristics of love. He says that love triumphs over all things and spiritual gifts. If one has the gift of prophecy, mystery, and knowledge, it is nothing and useless without love. If someone gives away their possessions to the poor and gives over their body, they are still nothing without love. Love is patient, love is kind. It does not envy, it does not boast, it is not proud. It does not dishonor others, it is not self-seeking, it is not easily angered, it keeps no record of wrongs. Love does not delight in evil but rejoices with the truth. It always protects, always trusts, always hopes, always perseveres. Prophecies will cease, languages disappear, knowledge will pass away, but love endures forever and never fails. Faith, hope, and love remain, but the greatest of these is love.

In chapter 14, Paul discusses intelligibility in worship. He says to follow the way of love and to eagerly desire gifts of the spirit, especially prophecy. People who speak in tongues are speaking to God and not to people because no one understands them, they utter mysteries by the spirit. The one who prophesies, speak to people for their strengthening, encouraging, and comfort. Paul encourages the Corinthians to seek the gift of prophecy, which he considers more beneficial for the church than speaking in tongues. Paul explains that speaking in tongues is useless because it is like speaking into the air. Unless they communicate words with an understandable message, then how will anyone know what they are saying. Paul calls for good order in worship. He gives instructions for what is appropriate regarding worship in church. God is not a God of disorder but of peace, as in all the congregations of the lord's people. Many people have spiritual experiences like a hymn, a word of instruction, a revelation, or an interpretation. Everything should be done in a fitting and orderly way. If someone wants to speak in tongues, then their needs to be an interpreter. Each speaker should have their words weighed carefully by the others. He says to speak in turn so that everyone may be instructed and encouraged. So that if an unbeliever comes in to inquire, they will see orderly prayer and will be convicted of sin and fall down to worship God.

In chapter 15, Paul's discusses is the resurrection of Christ and how it is the foundation of their belief. Some people within the church were saying there is no resurrection of the dead and insist that it is not really important. Paul reminds the Corinthians of the gospel they have received, which is founded on the death, burial, and resurrection of Jesus Christ. He says by this gospel, they are saved and if they do not hold onto his words firmly, then their belief is in vain. Jesus appeared to hundreds of eyewitnesses after his death, who were still alive at the time of Paul writing this. Christ died for the sins of the world and his resurrection was the ultimate defeat of death. The crucifixion and resurrection was the most important moment in human history because God poured his spirit into the world and only by God's grace, the price of death and sin was paid. Paul says that if there was no resurrection and Christ himself was not raised, then faith in him would be pointless. If Christ has not been raised, then preaching and faith is useless. But since Christ was raised, those who have died in Christ will also be resurrected. Paul says that will happen in a flash, in the twinkling of an eye, at the last trumpet. He prophesied that the trumpet will sound, the dead will be raised imperishable, and they will be changed. Thanks be to God because he gives the victory through the Lord Jesus Christ. Paul reminds them to give themselves fully to the work of the lord and their labor will not be in vain.

In chapter 16, Paul closes out the first letter to the Corinthians by giving instruction on how to prepare a special contribution for the lord's people. He emphasizes the need to set aside a sum of money in accordance with their income. He describes his travel plans and which ministry he will visit, communicating his intention to visit Corinth after passing through Macedonia. Also, he states his plans to stay at Ephesus until Pentecost and mentions to make sure to welcome Timothy because he is carrying on the lord's work. Paul gives encouragements to stand firm in the faith, to be courageous and strong, and to do everything in love. Paul sends greetings from the churches in Asia and affirms his love for all who love the lord. He ends with wishing the grace of the lord be with them.

2 Corinthians

Paul had multiple writings and an ongoing relationship with the community in Corinth. He started many churches and brought in many Jesus followers when he was on missionary trips. The first Corinthians is about Paul getting reports of things not going well within the church and giving instructions to correct them. In the second Corinthians, Paul has a painful visit and writes the letter with sorrow and tears. Paul shows he has only love for them and the lord, despite their sinful actions they are remorseful for. They overlooked Paul as a leader and looked down at him. He was poor, homeless, imprisoned frequently, and was not a good speaker. They were embarrassed of Paul because of his social status, but true honor of Jesus is not about self-promotion or rich social status. Paul shows the glory of Lord Jesus through his own suffering. Paul's life and leadership represents the crucified and resurrected Jesus.

In chapter 1, it is about suffering, comfort, and God's faithfulness. It starts out with Paul praising the God of all comfort. Grace and peace from God the Father and the Lord Jesus Christ. The father of compassion and the God of all comfort. He shares how they are comforted in their troubles so that they may also comfort those who are suffering. They rely on God's grace, and not worldly wisdom. Paul changes plans to postpone his visit to Corinth. He explains he does not want to come as planned because it would be too painful dealing with some of the sin they did. Paul says to forgive sin, so Satan does not outwit them. He praises God and stands firm on faith.

In chapter 2 -3, Paul compares the old covenant with God verses the new. The old was given to Moses and the new is about Jesus and the spirit. God has made ministers of the new covenant, with the spirit. The spirit gives life. The glory of the old covenant was so bright that the Israelites could not look Moses straight in the face. If they thought the old covenant was glorious, the new is so much more glorious and cannot compare. The glory of the new covenant is greater and brings righteousness. He says the new covenant is bold and filled with hope. The lord is the spirit, and where the spirit of the lord is, there is freedom.

In chapter 4, it shows what the cross reveals. It is about Jesus dying for the sins of the world. God is personal and suffering God, who brings new creation and life. He tells them to not lose heart because it is through God's mercy that they have this ministry. Those who believe have renounced their shameful ways. They do not use deception or distort the word of God. Even if the veil is uncovered, those who are perishing are unable to see the light of the gospel that displays the glory of Christ, who is the image of God. The minds of the unbelievers have been blinded. Paul compares them with a jar of clay, showing that this all-surpassing power is from God. Believers always carry around the death of Jesus in their body, so that the life of Jesus may also be revealed in their body. They are hard pressed on every side, persecuted, and struck down but never abandoned or destroyed. Those who are alive and die in the name of Jesus will be glorified, the one who raised Jesus will also raise them. Paul reminds the Corinthians not to lose heart because their troubles are light and temporary compared to the eternal glory that far outweighs them all. It is important to look to the spiritual world beyond the physical world. Although outwardly it may seem like they are wasting away, but inwardly they are being renewed day by day. Do not fix the eyes only on what can be seen, look for what is unseen. What is seen is temporary and the unseen is eternal.

In chapter 5, Paul refers to earthly bodies as tents that get destroyed, but a building from God is an eternal house in heaven. They groan and are burdened by their earthly bodies because they long to be in their heavenly dwelling. Paul states that Christ will judge everyone. Each person will receive what is due for the things they have done in the body, whether good or bad. He says they live by faith, not sight. Their goal is to please the lord, whether they are at home in the body or away from it. Christ's love compels them in their ministry because Christ's death was for all. All who live should no longer live for themselves but for him who died and was raised again. If anyone is in Christ, they are a new creation. The old worldly point of view has gone and the new is here. All this is from God, who reconciled people to himself through Christ and gave the ministry of reconciliation. Through Christ's sacrifice, they may be reconciled with God. God made him who had no sin to be sin for them, so that in him they might become the righteousness of God.

In chapter 6, Paul urges them to accept God's grace, and for them not to receive God's grace in vain. In the time of his favor, he heard them, and in the day of salvation he helped them, he tells them now is the time of God's favor and the day of salvation. He highlights their persistence and integrity. As servants of God, they commend themselves in every way with great endurance. They face troubles, hardships, distress, beatings, imprisonments, sleepless nights, and hunger. They do it in purity, understanding, patience and kindness, in the holy spirit and in sincere love. In truthful speech and in the power of God; with weapons of righteousness in the right hand and in the left. Through glory and dishonor, bad report and good report. They are genuine but appear as imposters, they are known but regarded as unknown, they are killed but live on, they are sorrowful yet always rejoicing, they are poor but making many rich, have nothing yet possess everything. This passage emphasizes that outward appearances are not representative of the true state of the heart and mission. Paul urges them to keep their hearts open. The chapter ends with him warning them against idolatry, and says to not be yoked together with unbelievers. Lightness and dark are incompatible and the righteous and the wicked do not have things in common, same way there is no harmony between Christ and Belial.

In chapter 7, Paul calls for holiness and love, he tells the Corinthians to purify themselves from everything that contaminates body and spirit, perfecting holiness out of reverence for God. Paul shares his joy over the church's repentance and talks about his love and pride in them. When they came into Macedonia, they were faced with harassment and hardships, but God comforted them through the arrival of Titus. Paul says he does not regret his letter, because it caused them sorrow which led to genuine repentance. He feels bad that the letter hurt them temporarily, but ultimately Godly sorrow brings repentance that leads to salvation and leaves no regret. Worldly sorrow brings death. Paul has complete confidence in them and says his spirit has been refreshed by all of them.

In chapter 8, it is about generosity and selflessness. Paul was raising money for Jewish Christians that were struggling and hit by famine. It says to strive for generosity that reaches beyond their means or circumstances, it is an example of Christ's sacrificial giving. Paul starts out by complimenting the church of Macedonia for their rich generosity and overflowing joy, despite being in the midst of severe trial and poverty. Paul testifies that they gave as much as they were able to, even beyond their ability. They did it entirely on their own, exceeding expectations and giving themselves to the lord first. Paul encourages the Corinthians to also excel in the grace of giving. He says that by the grace of the Lord Jesus Christ, that though he was rich, yet for their sake he became poor, so that through his poverty they might become rich. Also, that they should demonstrate their love for God through their actions, not just talk about giving, but act on it. He tells them to finish the work, so that their eager willingness may be matched by their completion of it, within their means. If the willingness is there, the gift is acceptable according to what someone has, not according to what they do not have. The one who gathered much did not have too much, and the one who gathered little did not have too little. This is about equality, those who generously share will be blessed.

In chapter 9, it continues on the topic of generosity. These chapters show the power of joyful and generous giving. It teaches that acts of giving should be with the intent of genuine love, not coming from a place of obligation. Whoever sows sparingly will also reap sparingly, and whoever sows generously will also reap generously. He insists that each person should give what they have decided in their heart, not reluctantly or under compulsion. God loves a cheerful giver. Paul assures them that God can bless them abundantly if they genuinely take care of others. Others will praise God for the obedience that accompanies their confession of the gospel of Christ, and for their generosity in sharing with them and with everyone else. They will be enriched in every way so they can be generous on every occasion. This is an indescribable gift given by the grace of God.

In chapter 10, it talks about spiritual battles and Paul defends his apostolic authority. The Corinthians are missing the message of Jesus when they look down on Paul. He says that the war he fights is not worldly, and the weapons they fight with are not weapons of this world. They have power to demolish strongholds. They dismantle arguments and every claim that sets itself up against the knowledge of God, and they take captive every thought and make it obedient to Christ. They judge Paul based off appearances on what they perceive as weakness, but Paul says anyone who is confident they belong to Christ should reconsider. He says his authority given by the lord is for lifting people up, not tearing them down. He declares that he will not boast beyond limits but will only boast within the area God assigned to him. His hope is that their faith continues to grow.

In chapter 11, Paul continues to defend his apostolic authority and expresses his concern for the Corinthians, who are being led by false teachers. He never charged any money to spread the gospel because his service was selfless, unlike the false apostles who preached for profit. There are these so-called super apostles who think they are superior based off worldly things. Paul's duty is to bring the bride of believers to the husband Christ, and he is concerned that the cunning serpent of evil may lead them astray. Paul will boast gladly about his weaknesses, so that Christ's power may glorified through him. That is why he delights in weaknesses, in insults, in hardships, in persecutions, and in difficulties. Paul was exposed to death so many times, beaten with lashes and sometimes rods, pelted with stones, spent days on the open sea always on the move, constantly in danger from rivers, bandits, jews, and gentiles. He has gone without sleep, gone without food and water, and have been cold and naked. On top of all that, he faces daily pressure of his concern for churches. But these Corinthians call Paul weak because of his appearance, Paul says he does not feel weak. The chapter is a warning against false teachers that lead people away from gospel, and says no wonder Satan masquerades as an angel of light. He is not surprised his servants masquerade as servants of righteousness.

In chapter 12, Paul describes a vision of a thorn in his flesh. This describes how God's power is manifested through Paul's weakness. He took this thorn as a message from Satan to torment him, and when Paul cried out the lord said, "my grace is sufficient for you, for my power is made perfect in weakness." This helped him understand what it means to be humble and how much he relies on God's grace. In his most helpless moments, Christ is his strength. Paul explains that his words and actions are for them to grow spiritually and mature. Paul's life is an example of how an apostle should be through weakness and suffering like Christ, not through boasting and power like the false teachers.

In chapter 13, Paul gives a final warning for them to self-reflect on what it means to follow Christ. He encourages the Corinthians to examine and test themselves to see if they are in the faith, and that Jesus Christ lives in them. Christ was crucified in weakness, yet lives in God's power. Same way they are weak, yet by God's power they live. Despite Paul's harsh and authoritative words, he prays for their restoration. The authority the lord gave him is to build them up, not to tear them down. He is concerned about their spiritual growth and sends his final blessings assuring them of Christ's grace, God's love, and the fellowship of the holy spirit. He says to strive for full restoration, encourage one another, be of one mind, and to live in peace. Lastly, wishing for the God of love and peace to be with them.

Galatians

Galatia was a Roman province in central Asia Minor. Paul traveled here on each of the three journeys he made to spread the good news of Jesus. Some people, who Paul calls agitators, came and challenged his leadership as well as the foundation of his teachings. This letter is an answer to the threat of his status as an apostle and reaffirm his message, which is that belief in Jesus is the basis of membership in these new communities. In this letter, Paul is concerned about the controversy surrounding gentile Christians not following mosaic law or the torah, specifically circumcision. Paul argues that gentile Galatians do not need to adhere to every mosaic law, the more important thing is to accept Jesus Christ as their lord and savior. The law is part of the old covenant and was not enough to overcome sin and death.

In chapter 1, Paul starts out by saying his authority did not come from men nor by a man, but by Jesus Christ and God the Father. He reminds them of Jesus' self-sacrifice, who gave his life for the sins of the world, to rescue them from the present evil age, according to the will of God the Father. He is astonished that evidently some people are perverting the gospel of Christ, they are deserting the one who called them to live in the grace of Christ and turning to a different gospel, which is really no gospel at all. He states that if anyone preaches a gospel that is contrary to the one that was preached, even if they are an angel from heaven, they will be under God's curse. Paul says he does not seek human approval, only God's approval. If he were trying to please people, then he would not be a servant of Christ. He says he wants them to know that the gospel he preaches is not of human origin. He did not receive it from any man, nor was he taught it. He received it by revelation from Jesus Christ. Paul reminds them of his past life in Judaism, about how intensely he persecuted the church of God and tried to destroy it. God set him apart from his mother's womb and called him by his grace and revealed his son in him, so that he may preach among the gentiles. He said his immediate response was not to consult other human beings, he went into Arabia and later returned to Damascus. Then after three years he went to Jerusalem but was personally unknown in the churches of Judea that are in Christ. They only knew Paul by the news or report, about how the former prosecutor is now preaching the faith he once tried to destroy. They praised God because of him.

In chapter 2, Paul originally spoke with the other apostles like Peter and James about circumcision not being required as well as other Jewish laws, which they said they were in support of. Peter went to Antioch to see the non-Jewish Christians and when Jerusalem opposition came to Antioch, he began to draw back and cave under pressure. He distanced himself and stopped eating with gentile Christians. Paul accuses Peter of hypocrisy for not staying true to the gospel. Initially, Peter eats with gentile believers, but withdraws when some men with James arrive, fearing those of the circumcision group. Other Jewish Christians, including Barnabas follow Peters hypocrisy, which led Paul to confront Peter about not living in line with the truth of the gospel. He called out Cephas in front of everyone asking how it is possible he is a Jew who lives like a gentile, and are not like Jew yet forces gentiles to follow Jewish customs. Paul said, we who are Jews by birth and not sinful gentiles know that a person is not justified by the words of the law or torah, but rather by the faith in Jesus Christ. So, they too have put their faith in Jesus Christ so that they may be justified by faith in Christ and not by works of the law, because the works of the law no one will be justified. He clarifies that this absolutely does not justify or promote sin, it is through the law he died to the law so that he may live for God. It is only through Jesus giving his life, that they may be saved by grace because if righteousness could be gained through law, then Christ died for nothing.

In chapter 3, it sends a message about the priority of faith in a relationship with God. It emphasizes that they are saved not through works of the law, but by faith in Jesus Christ. Paul says it is foolish to believe they could achieve salvation through human effort of flesh. He reminds them of Jesus' crucifixion and asks whether they received the spirit through works of the law or if they received it through faith in Jesus. Abraham believed in God, so it was credited to him as righteousness. All who have faith are children of Abraham. Scripture predicted that God would justify the gentiles by faith and announced the gospel in advance to Abraham. All nations would be blessed through him so that those who rely on faith are blessed along with Abraham, a man of faith. It is prophesied in the old testament that the ones who rely on the works of the law are under a curse. All fail to keep the laws perfectly, so no one can be justified righteous. God is beyond space and time; he always knew that the law would be a temporary action. It exposed the sins of the world; they constantly rebelled against God's law. The law was added because of transgressions until the promised seed had come. Ultimately, according to the law, Israel and the whole world stand guilty of sin. The laws imprisoned everyone under the power of sin. The law was a guardian leading the world to Christ, his crucifixion paid the price for the guilty sin, and now the world is justified through faith. Now that this faith has come, they are no longer under a guardian. God in his grace made a divine promise and gave it to Abraham. The law cannot alter the covenant God duly established, the promise given to Abraham and his seed stands. Scripture does not use plural seeds, it uses a singular seed meaning one person, who is Christ. If someone belongs to Christ, then they are Abraham's seed, and are heirs according to the promise. So, in Christ Jesus, everyone who believes is children of God through faith.

In chapter 4, Paul uses an analogy by comparing heirs to slaves. As long as someone is underage, they are under the ownership of their parents, and the heir is subject to guardians and trustees until the time set by their parents. When humans were underage, they were in slavery under the elemental spiritual forces of the world. But when the set time had fully come, God sent his son to redeem those under the law so that they might receive adoption to sonship. Since humans are God's children, he sent the spirit of his son into the hearts of the world. So, they are no longer a slave, but God's child who God has made an heir. Paul has his concerns for the Galatians. He reminds them of their previous idol worship and how they were slaves to those who by nature are not gods. He asks how they could turn back to those weak and miserable forces. He is fearful that his efforts may have been wasted on them. They welcomed him despite his illness when he first preached the gospel to them. Paul tells them that false teachers are leading them off track. He said these false teachers are enthusiastically trying to alienate and win them over with bad intentions. Paul considers Galatians like his own children who he is trying to mature in their faith in God.

In the last section of chapter four, it makes a reference to Sarah and Hagar, who were Abraham's first two sons mothers. One is a slave woman, and the other is a free woman. His son with the slave woman was born according to flesh, and his son with the free woman was born as a result of a divine promise. The women represent two covenants, one is from Mount Sanai and bears children who are to be slaves of law, this is Hagar. Hagar stands for Mount Sinai in Arabia and corresponds to the present city of Jerusalem, because she is in slavery with her children. Hagars story can be interpreted to reveal hidden meaning. It symbolizes the Mosaic covenant, which is subject to bondage under the law, and emphasizes the difference between trying to obtain salvation by works verses achieving it through faith and grace. Those who trust in Christ are free from bondage of the law and are children of the free woman Sarah. They are the children of a divine promise through her son Isaac.

In chapter 5, it says it is for freedom that Christ sets people free. Those who live by the whole law and obligated to obey the law are living as though Christ was not killed for the sins of the world and fulfill God's divine promise. Some Jews question how gentiles are able to understand God's laws, but the key is the spirit of Jesus. They were called to be free. Paul says to not use the freedom to indulge in the flesh, instead use the freedom to serve one another humbly in love. The entire law is fulfilled in keeping this one command, love your neighbor as yourself. It says to walk in spirit and stay away from gratifying the desires of the flesh. Fleshly desires are contrary to the spirit and are in conflict with each other, so someone cannot just do whatever they want. If the spirit leads someone, they are not under law. The acts of the flesh are obvious including sexual immorality, impurity and debauchery; idolatry and witchcraft; hatred, discord, jealousy, fits of rage, selfish ambition, dissensions, faction, envy, drunkenness, orgies, and more like this. Those who live like this will not inherit the kingdom of God. On the other hand, the fruit of the spirit is love, joy, peace, patience, kindness, goodness, faithfulness, gentleness and self-control. Against such things there is no law. Those who belong to Christ Jesus have crucified the flesh with its passions and desires. Paul says to keep in step with the spirit, since they live by spirit. Also to not become conceited, provoking and envying each other.

In chapter 6, Paul writes about doing good for all. If somebody is caught in a sin, then a person living in spirit should restore that person gently but be careful because they could be tempted into sin themselves. They fulfill the law of Christ when they carry each other's burdens. If anyone acts like someone they are not, they are only deceiving themselves. Each person should evaluate their own life and actions without comparing themselves to others. It emphasizes self-reflection and personal responsibility. Each person shall carry their own load because a man reaps what he sows. It says to not be deceived because God cannot be mocked. Whoever sows to please their flesh, from the flesh will reap destruction; whoever sows to please the spirit, from the spirit will reap eternal life. Do not become weary in doing good because as long as someone does not give up, a proper time will come when a harvest will be reaped. Do good to all people, especially to those who belong to the family of believers. Paul finishes off the last chapter writing about the new creation. There is a constant debate on circumcision, and some are getting circumcised just to avoid persecution. Paul says neither circumcision nor uncircumcision means anything; what counts is the new creation. The only thing worth boasting is in the cross of the Lord Jesus Christ, through which the world has been crucified. Paul bears the marks of Jesus and has been justified by faith in Christ and what was accomplished on the cross. Paul no longer needs the approval of the world. Then the letter ends with him wishing the grace of the Lord Jesus Christ be with their spirit

Ephesians

Ephesians was a city in ancient Greece that was taken over by Romans. Ephesians is mentioned in acts, and they held the name Jesus in high honor because of the missionary work Paul did over there. Paul writes this letter from jail. It is about how the gospel must be applied to one's personal life, and about the new identity believers have in Christ. God has elevated Jesus above all things, and created one new humanity with all people around the world, with Christ as the head Paul says people will enter a spiritual battle and must arm themselves with all the resources God has provided, until Jesus brings unity to all things in heaven and on earth.

In chapter 1, starts out with a poem honoring God the Father and what he has done in Christ. Through forgiveness and grace, he chose for humanity to be saved. God predestined them for adoption to sonship through Jesus Christ in accordance with his pleasure and will. It praises God's glorious grace, which he has freely given in the one he loves. In him there is redemption through his blood, forgiveness of sins, in accordance with the riches of God's grace. God has made known the mystery of his will through Christ, to be put in effect when times reach fulfillment, to bring unity to all things in heaven and on earth. It says when a person believes, they are marked with a seal, which is the promised holy spirit. In him they have been predestined, according to God's plans and will. Paul prays to the glorious father that they may get to know him better and the eyes of their heart be enlightened, so they may know the hope that had been called to them, his glorious inheritance in his holy people. He prays for believers to experience and know God's incomparable great power, that power is the same power that raised Christ from the dead and seated him at the right hand in the heavenly realms. He is above all rule and authority for all ages past, present, and future. God placed all things under his feet and appointed him to be head over everything for the church, which his body, the fulness of him who fills everything in every way.

In chapter 2, it is about being made alive in Christ. They were dead in their transgressions and sins, in which they followed the ways of the world, gratifying the cravings of the sinful flesh, following its desires and thoughts. Like all of humanity, by nature they deserve wrath and judgement. But because God is rich in mercy and has great love for humans, he has made them alive in Christ even when they were already dead in transgressions. Paul says it is by faith and grace they are saved, expressed in the kindness of Christ. It cannot be achieved through works; it is a gift from God. The laws of the Torah has been fulfilled through Jesus and he himself is peace, who has destroyed the barrier between Jew and gentile. The old covenant had a limited barrier, but the new covenant fulfilled God's promise to unite a new humanity. Everyone who has faith in Jesus are fellow citizens with God's people and also members of the household. In him the whole building is joined together and rises to become a holy temple in the lord. All believers are built together in which God lives by his spirit.

In chapter 3, it is about God's plan to unify all through Christ. Paul writes this as a prisoner for the sake of the gentiles. He discusses his role as a minister of the gospel, made possible by God's grace. His purpose is to display God's wisdom through the church. Other generations did not understand the mystery of God's plan, but now the it has now been revealed by the spirit to God's holy apostles and prophets. This mystery is that through the gospel the gentiles are heirs together with Israel, members together of one body, and sharers together in the promise in Christ Jesus. Paul tells them to not be discouraged by his sufferings, through faith in the lord they may approach God with freedom and confidence. Paul prays for the Ephesians, asking God to strengthen them with power through the spirit in their inner being, and for Christ to dwell in their hearts through faith. He prays that they may know the deep love of Christ and his limitless dimensions. He prays for them to be filled with all the fullness of God, to be rooted and established in love, and know this love surpasses knowledge. God is able to do immeasurably more than one could ask or imagine for.

In chapter 4, it is about the unity and maturity in the body of Christ. Oneness is the key message in this chapter, one body unified by one spirit, one lord, one faith, one baptism. There is one God and Father of all, who is over all, and through all, and in all. Each believer has been given grace which has been given as Christ appointed it. God gives spiritual gifts to the saints, the prophets, the evangelists, the pastors, and teachers, to equip his people for works of service, so that the body of Christ may be built up towards unity and maturity. Unity in the faith and in the knowledge of the son of God. When speaking the truth about love and Christ, they will grow and mature in every respect so that they may no longer be like infants being deceived by schemers and liars, who toss people back and forth with false teachings in their cunning and crafty ways. From him the whole body, joined and held together by every supporting ligament, grows and builds itself up in love, as each part does its work. Paul gives instructions on how to live as a follower of Jesus. He teaches to put off the old self and former ways that has been corrupted by deceitful desires, and to be made new in the attitude of their minds and to put on the new self, created to be like God in true righteousness and holiness. The old self is darkened in their understanding and separated from the life of God because of the ignorance that is in them due to the hardening of their hearts. They are so far gone and lost all sensitivity to moral standards. They give themselves over to every pleasurable desire and indulge in every kind of impurity, full of greed. He says they must put off falsehood and speak truthfully to their neighbor, because all are members of one body. Paul advises against falsehood, uncontrolled rage and anger, stealing, unwholesome talk, brawling, slander, bitterness, and malice. Instead, he says to be kind and compassionate to one another, forgiving each other as God forgave them.

In chapter 5, it shows how to apply the gospel to one's own life and live a Christ centered lifestyle. He says to walk in the way of love, just as Christ loved the world and gave himself as a sacrifice. He warns against immoral behaviors such as sexual immorality, impurity, greed, foolish talk, obscenity, or idolatry. These things are improper for God's people, and they will not have inheritance in the kingdom of God. As transformed believers, they are encouraged to live as children of light. Before they were in darkness but are now light in the lord. They are to have nothing to do with the fruitless deeds of darkness, but rather expose them. Everything exposed by the light becomes visible, this is why it is said, "wake up sleeper, rise from the dead, and Christ will shine on you." He warns to be careful how they live and to make the most of every opportunity, because the days are evil. Do not be foolish. Live by the lord's will. Be filled with the spirit, express faith with songs making music from the heart to the lord. Give thanks always to God the Father for everything and in the name of the Lord Jesus Christ. In the final part of chapter five, Paul gives instructions to husbands and wives, comparing their relationship to Christ and the church. Wives are to submit to their husbands, and husbands are to love their wives just as Christ loved the church. As written in Genesis, a man will leave his father and mother and be united to his wife, and the two will become one flesh.

In chapter 6, Paul discusses the truth about spiritual warfare, telling believers to put on the full armor of God, so they can take a stand against the devil's schemes. Struggle is not against flesh and blood, but against the rulers, against the authorities, against the powers of this dark world and against the spiritual forces of evil in the heavenly realms. Therefore, put on the full armor of God so that when the day of evil comes, they may be able to stand their ground. To be able to stand firm with the belt of truth buckled around the waist and a breastplate of righteousness, with feet standing ready that comes from the gospel of peace. In addition to all this, take up the shield of faith, with which they can extinguish all the flaming arrows of the evil one. Take the helmet of salvation and the sword of the spirit, which is the word of God. Be alert and always keep on praying for all the lord's people. He concludes the letter with encouragement, sending his final greeting about faith, love, and grace to all who love the Lord Jesus Christ. Paul emphasizes the need for constant prayer so he can fearlessly make known the mystery of the gospel.

Philippians

Paul helped start a church in the city of Phillipi and it was one of the first Jesus communities in Europe. It was a colony of Roman soldiers who became Paul's friends and supporters, helping collect money to assist him in prison. He knew they were experiencing a lot of opposition and uses his own life as an example of how to respond to hardship and joy. Paul did not boast about the high position he had and humbled himself up until his death. This is the new way how humans should be, that is revealed in God's kingdom, urging others to have the same servant mentality Jesus had.

In chapter 1, it starts out with a prayer of gratefulness for the Philippians generosity and faithfulness. Paul and Timothy greet the believers in Philippi, expressing their gratitude for them and praying for their spiritual growth. Paul says they are in his heart since day one and prays with joy for their partnerships in the gospel until now. Whether he is in chains or defending the gospel, all of them share in God's grace with him. He prays that their love may abound more and more in knowledge and depth of insight, so that they may be able to discern what is best, and be blameless on the day of Christ. Paul shares about his imprisonment, explaining that it has actually served to advance the gospel. It has become clear to everyone that he is in chains for Christ, and because of his chains, many brothers and sisters have become confident in the lord and dare all the more to proclaim the gospel without fear. Some preach Christ out of selfish ambition, but others out of goodwill. The ones who do it of goodwill do so out of love, knowing that he was put here for the defense of the gospel. Regardless of their motivations, Paul rejoices that Christ is preached. Christ will be exalted in his body whether by life or by death. Paul is torn between the two of life and death because he wants be with Jesus in the afterlife. If he desires to depart then he will be with Christ which is better by far, but it is more necessary that he remains in the body. Paul is confident he will remain and continue to help them grow in their faith. Paul says whatever happens, to conduct themselves in a manner worthy of the gospel of Christ. So even in his absence, he will know they stand firm in one spirit, striving together as one for the faith of the gospel. He says to not be afraid of those that oppose, they will be saved by God, and it is a sign to them that opposition will be destroyed. For it has been granted to them on behalf of Christ not only to believe in him, but also to suffer for him.

In chapter 2, it is a call to imitate Christ's humility. Paul encourages the believers to strive for unity, humility, selflessness, and to value others above themselves. It says to be of one spirit and one of one mind, do nothing out of selfish ambition or vain pride. In relationships with one another, have the same mindset as Jesus. Christ was the ultimate example of humility, who being in very nature God, never used his equality with God for his own advantage. Instead he made himself nothing by taking the form of a servant, being made in human likeness. He was found in appearance as a man, he humbled himself by becoming obedient to death, even death on a cross for the sins of the world. Therefore, God exalted him to the highest place and gave him the name that is above every name, and every tongue will acknowledge that Jesus Christ is Lord, to the glory of God the Father. In the next section of the chapter it says to do everything without complaining or grumbling. Continue to work out salvation by applying God's grace to their daily lives, for it is God who works in them in order to fulfill his good purpose. The ones who are blameless and pure in a warped and crooked generation will shine like stars in the sky. Hold firmly to the word of life, so that God can boast on the day of Christ. The chapter ends with Paul talking about Timothy and Epaphroditus, who are living out their life in the example of Christ.

Timothy is known for his genuine care and concern for others, and Epaphroditus risked his life for the work of Christ. These two people's lives are representations of what it means to live for Christ and says to honor people like them.

In chapter 3, it starts out with a warning against false teachers. Paul says to watch out for those dogs, evildoers, and mutilators of flesh. He teaches that true believers worship God in the spirit, rejoice in Christ Jesus, and put no confidence in the flesh. He emphasizes the greatness of knowing Christ over earthly and religious credentials. Paul said he was a pharisee and lived righteously under the law, which he says are worthless compared to knowing the Lord Jesus. He is willing to lose all things in order to gain Christ and to be found in him, through faith Jesus. To know Christ is to know the power of his resurrection and participation in his sufferings, and to become like him in death. He presses on toward the ultimate prize of eternal life in Christ in heaven. Many live as enemies of the cross of Christ and their destiny is destruction. Paul says their God is in their stomach and their mind is set on earthly things. Their citizenship is in heaven while they eagerly await for the return of the Lord Jesus, who has the power to bring everything under his control and will transform ordinary bodies into glorious ones.

In chapter 4, Paul makes closing appeals for steadfast faith and unity. He says to stand firm in the lord and to let their gentleness be evident to all, for the lord is near. It says to not be anxious about anything and to present their requests to God in every situation through prayer and thanks. The peace of God transcends all understanding and will guide the minds and hearts in Jesus Christ. Whatever learned, received, or heard from Paul should be put it into practice and the peace of God will be with them. Paul thanks them for their gifts in his time of need. He describes how believers can overcome worry and worldly desires regardless of the circumstances. He shares his secret to being content in all circumstances, whether well-fed or hungry, whether living in plenty or in want. He can do all things through Christ who gives him strength. God can provide all needs according to the riches of his glory in Christ Jesus, do not be consumed by materialism or anxiety. He sends his final greeting and prays for the grace of the Lord Jesus Christ be with their spirit.

Colossians

Colossians is a letter written to believers in the city of Colossae, Paul was in prison awaiting his trial in Rome before Caesar. The people in Colossae were mostly gentiles, and some people were spreading false teaching and adding extra rules. Paul says that all things in heaven and earth were created by God, and Jesus death on the cross brought in the new kingdom of God.

In chapter 1, Paul and Timothy greet the holy and faithful brothers and sisters in Colossae, wishing grace and peace from God. Epaphras, who is a faithful minister of Christ brought the gospel to the people in Colossae and started the church. Paul writes this letter from prison and prays for their faith, hope, and love. He prays for their spiritual wisdom and understanding to live a life worthy of the lord, bearing fruit in every good work and growing in the knowledge of God. Giving joyful thanks to the Father, who has qualified them to share in the inheritance of his holy people in the kingdom of light. He has rescued them from the dominion of darkness and brought them into the kingdom of the son he loves, where they have redemption and the forgiveness of sins. Paul declares the supremacy of the son of God. Jesus is in the image of God and the firstborn over all creation. In him all things were created, in heaven and on earth, visible and invisible. All things were created through him, and for him. He is before all things, and in him all things are held together. The church is the body and Christ is the head. God was pleased to have his fullness dwell in him, and is the source of all creation, making peace through his blood shed on the cross. Paul reminds them that humans were once alienated from God and were enemies in their minds because of evil behavior, but now have been reconciled through Christ's death. He encourages them to continue in faith, established and firm and do not move from the hope held out in the gospel. The mystery that has been kept hidden for ages and generations is now disclosed to the lord's people. God has chosen to make himself known among the gentiles, the glorious riches of this mystery, which is Christ in them, the hope of glory. Paul rejoices in his suffering for the sake of the church, which is the body of Christ. He has become a servant by the commission of God and Paul's hardships only further spread the message of the gospel; it is not a burden but a privilege to share in Christ's work. Maturing in Christ as a way of life is the goal, proclaiming, admonishing and teaching everyone with all wisdom.

In chapter 2, it is about of the wholeness and freedom that come from living in Christ. His goal is for them to be encouraged in heart and united in love, so they may have the full riches of complete understanding, so they can know the mystery of God. Hidden treasures of wisdom and knowledge are known through Christ. He tells them this so that no one can deceive them with fine-tuned and nice sounding arguments against God's existence. Although Paul is physically absent, he says he is with them in spirit and delighted to see how disciplined and firm their faith in Christ is. Paul instructs the them to continue living their lives in Christ just as they were taught, and always be overflowing with thankfulness. Christ is the head over every power and authority, and tells them to let no one lead them astray through hollow and deceptive philosophy. Focus on Christ rather than human traditions and elemental spiritual forces. Paul said the spiritual circumcision done by Christ, through which they were buried with him in baptism and raised with him through faith. Humans were dead in sin, but God made them alive with Christ by forgiving the world for all sins. The wages of sin is death and Jesus being nailed on the cross paid that price, cancelling the legal debt, to which humanity stood condemned. Jesus disarmed the powers and authorities, he made a public spectacle of them, triumphing over them by the cross.

The last part of chapter two, Paul discusses freedom from human rules. He tells the Colossians not to let anyone judge them based on what they eat, drink, or religious festivals they observe. Also, to not let anyone who delights in false humility and the worship of angels disqualify them. These people are puffed up with preconceived notions in their unspiritual mind. A believer in Christ is no longer part of this world and do not need to submit to its rules because it is based on mere human commands and teachings. Such regulations have an appearance of wisdom but lack any value. He warns to not be convinced by false teachings or rules disconnected from Christ.

In chapter 3, it is about new life and a new humanity with Christ, putting the old self to death. Paul urges believers to set their minds and hearts on things above, not earthly things. Their lives are now with Christ in God, so when Christ appears, they too will appear with him in glory. They are made alive in Christ. One should put to death their earthly nature such as sexual immorality, impurity, lust, evil desires and greed, and idolatry. The wrath of God is coming. Paul urges them to rid themselves of the life they once lived, and to rid themselves of anger, rage, malice, slander, and filthy language from the lips. Do not lie to each other, since they have taken off the old self and its practices and put on the new self, which is being renewed in knowledge in the image of the creator. Here there is no gentile or Jew, circumcised or uncircumcised, slave or free, because Christ is all, and is in all. Paul said as God's chosen people, holy and dearly loved, to clothe themselves with compassion, kindness, humility, gentleness and patience. Bear with each other and forgive one another, as the lord forgave them. Above all virtues is love which binds them together in perfect unity. Let the peace of Christ be in the heart, and as members of one body, it is called upon for peace and to be thankful. Sing to God with gratitude in the heart through psalms, hymns, and songs from the spirit. Do it all in the name of Lord Jesus, giving thanks to God the Father through him**.** The chapter ends with Paul giving instructions for Christian households. Wives are to submit to their husbands, as is fitting in the lord. Husbands are to love their wives and not be harsh with them. Children are to obey their parents, for it pleases the lord. Fathers are to not become bitter or resentful to their children, they will become discouraged. The passage acknowledges slaves and tells them whatever they do, it should be done with all their heart working for the lord and not for human masters. They will receive an inheritance from the lord in heaven because it is the lord they are serving. Anyone who does wrong will be repaid for their wrongs because there is no favoritism. In God's kingdom everyone has equal opportunity.

In chapter 4, it gives further instructions and final greetings. Paul encourages the Colossians to stay devoted in prayer, being watchful and thankful. He requests prayers for himself too, seeking guidance from God in preaching the mystery of Christ, so he can proclaim it clearly. Believers are advised to be wise in the way they act towards outsiders, making the most out of every opportunity. He emphasizes the importance of how someone should conduct themselves in conversations, it should be always filled with grace, seasoned with salt, so they may know how to answer anyone. Tychicus, a faithful minister and fellow servant in the lord is sent to deliver letters so he may encourage their hearts. Tychicus comes with Onesimus, an escaped slave to Philemon. Paul asks the Colossians to welcome Onesimus as an equal and beloved brother in the lord. The apostle asks Philemon to accept Onesimus back, not as a slave but as a believer and a brother in Christ. Paul said he wrote this greeting with his own hand and to remember his chains, and for grace to be with them.

1 Thessalonians

This letter is one of Paul's first letters. Paul, Timothy, and Silas brought the message about the good news of Jesus to the city of Thessalonica. Many people became believers and there was a riot when Paul and Silas were accused of defying Caesars decrees. They narrowly escaped and had to flee for their lives. Paul was concerned the believers in Thessalonica may become discouraged or led astray because of the opposition they were facing. Paul sent Timothy to encourage them and was happy to hear that the Thessalonians remained faithful.

In chapter 1, it is about faithfulness and thanksgiving. Paul, Silas and Timothy wish grace and peace upon church of the Thessalonians in the name of God the Father and the Lord Jesus Christ. The Thessalonians were being severely persecuted but still respond with joy and continue to prosper, showing their transformation and dedication, suffering just like the apostles and Jesus did. Paul recounts their conversion and describes how the Thessalonians turned away from idols to serve the true God. They live their life in hope waiting for Jesus's return who was raised from the dead because only he can save from the coming wrath.

In chapter 2, Paul said they were bold in bringing the gospel to Thessalonica in the face of strong opposition and being insulted in Philippi. They were not motivated by deceit, impure motives, or any tricks. They never used flattery or put on a mask to cover greed, with God as their witness. They are entrusted with the gospel and are not interested in pleasing people, only God who knows their hearts. Paul compares the Thessalonians to a mother caring for her young children and expresses his deep love for them. He encourages them to live lives worthy of God, who calls them into his kingdom and glory. Paul expresses his thanks to God continually because the Thessalonians received his message, they did not accept it as the word of men, but as the true word of God. This led them to experience persecution from their own people, just as the churches in Judea had suffered at the hands of the Jews, who killed the Lord Jesus, and the prophets, and drove out the apostles. They displease God and are hostile to everyone, the wrath of God will finally come upon them. Paul longs to revisit the Thessalonians but Satan blocked the way. It says their hope and joy is the glory in the presence of the Lord Jesus.

In chapter 3, it shows the importance of prayer and endurance in communities, and emphasizes the importance of faith, encouragement, and steadfastness during hardships. Paul longed to see them in person, and they longed to see him too. Paul was concerned for the Thessalonian believers and the impact the persecutions were going to have on the church. Timothy returned with good that they remained steadfast in faith, which brought comfort to Paul. He prays that the lord may strengthen their love, and overflow for each other and for everyone else. May he strengthen hearts so that they can be blameless and holy in the presence of God the Father, when the Lord Jesus comes with all his holy ones.

In chapter 4, Paul urges the Thessalonians to live a life that pleases God. These instructions are by the authority of the Lord Jesus. It is God's will that they should be sanctified and should avoid sexual immorality. Paul calls on believers to be sexually pure and learn to control the body in a way that is holy and honorable, not to just fall into passionate lust like the pagans did. No one should take advantage of a brother or sister, the lord will punish those who commit such sins, they have been warned before. God called on humans to live a holy life, not to be impure. Anyone who rejects these instructions are not rejecting humans; they are rejecting God who gave his holy spirit. It says it is good to live a quiet life and mind your own business.

Also it is good to have the ability to work with the hands, it will win the respect of outsiders and will not have to be dependent on anybody. Then the next section talks about the dead in Christ. He says he does not want them to be uniformed on the fate of souls or what happens to those sleeping in death. He does not want them to have no hope and grieve like the rest of mankind. When the day of the lord comes and Jesus returns, those who are still alive on earth will not precede the believers in Christ who are already dead. In these last days, the lord himself will come down from heaven, accompanied with an archangel, and with a loud command and trumpet call of God, the dead in Christ will rise first. After that, the believers who are still on earth will be caught up in the air and be with the lord forever. Therefore, encourage one another with these words.

In chapter 5, it goes into further detail about the day of the lord. The day of wrath and the great tribulation, nobody knows the time or hour, but they do know this day will come like a thief in the night. It says when you hear people talking about "peace and safety," that's when destruction will come suddenly, like labor pains on a pregnant woman. Those awaiting the lord's return should be armed with faith and love, and the hope of salvation as a helmet. Believers are children of light and of day, not darkness and night, so do not fall asleep. Be aware and alert for the day the lord returns. God did not appoint them just to suffer; it was so they can receive salvation through the Lord Jesus Christ. He died so they may live together with him, whether awake or asleep. Encourage one another and build each other up. Paul tells them to live in peace with each other and gives final instructions. He says to warn those who are idle and disruptive, encourage the disheartened, help the weak, and be patient with everyone. Always strive to do what is good for one another and everyone else, do not pay back a wrong with another wrong. Rejoice always and pray continually. Give thanks in all circumstances, God will be with them. Reject all forms of evil and cling to what is good. He prays for them to be sanctified by the God of peace and for their whole spirit, soul, and body be blameless on the day Lord Jesus Christ returns. He wishes the grace of the lord be with them all.

2 Thessalonians

Shortly after Paul wrote his first letter to the Thessalonians, he got a report that the persecutions continued. The Thessalonians were confused about the second coming of Christ, and started debating whether it is an event that already passed or a future event. He had to write a second letter to clarify the day of the lord is yet to come and they did not miss it.

In chapter 1, Paul, Silvanus, and Timothy greet the church of the Thessalonians, wishing grace and peace to them from God the Father and the Lord Jesus Christ. The love they express for one another and their faith is growing more and more each day. They have perseverance despite the trials and persecution they endure, and they thank God for that. God's judgement is always right and the believers who suffer for the lord will be counted as worthy of the kingdom of God. It encourages believers to endure and have faith that God's justice will prevail in the end, and the glory of Jesus will be revealed. God is just and those who cause trouble will face their judgement, he will grant relief to those who are troubled. This will happen when the Lord Jesus is revealed from heaven in blazing fire with his powerful angels. He will bring retribution on those who do not know God and disobey the gospel. Those who chose to live their life apart from God will be shut out of his presence for eternity. On the day the lord returns, he will be glorified and admired by believers and his holy people. Paul prays in the name of Jesus that they may be glorified in him and worthy of his calling, that with God's power he may bring to fruition their every desire for goodness.

In chapter 2, it further clarifies what the day of the lord means. The man of lawlessness, or what some may refer to as the anti-Christ is discussed. Paul says to not be easily unsettled or alarmed by teachers who claim that day of the lord has already come, it has not. He says to not let anyone deceive them in any way, the day of judgement will not come until the rebellion occurs and the man of lawlessness is revealed, the man doomed to destruction. He will oppose and will exalt himself over everything that is called God or is worshiped, he will set himself up in God's temple and proclaim to be God himself. The man of lawlessness is restrained, so that he may be revealed at the proper time. The coming of the lawless one will be in accordance with how Satan works. He will display his power using all sorts of signs and wonders that serve his lies. He will use all kinds of wickedness and deception so people may not be saved, those who refuse the truth and love of Jesus will perish. When the lawless one is revealed, the Lord Jesus will overthrow him with just a breathe of his mouth and destroy him. Jesus will triumph and achieve ultimate victory over evil. The secret power of the lawlessness is already at work and will continue to do so until he is taken out of the way. Those who have delighted in wickedness and not believed the truth will be condemned. The final verses in the chapter is a closing prayer of encouragement to stay thankful and hopeful. He says to stand firm in the glory of the Lord Jesus Christ, he has called upon them as first fruits to be saved through the sanctifying work of the spirit, through belief in the truth. He says to stand firm and hold onto the teachings of the gospel, may the Lord Jesus and God the Father give eternal encouragement, and hope by his grace, and may he encourage their heart and strengthen them.

In chapter 3, is a reminder of the importance of community, discipline, and hard work when living a Christian life. Paul requests the Thessalonians pray that the message of the lord be spread rapidly and be honored, and to pray they are delivered from wicked and evil people, because not everyone has faith. When the Lord is faithful, he will deliver and strengthen them from the evil one, and may the lord direct their hearts into God's love and Christs perseverance.

Paul provides guidelines to living responsibly within a community of believers, and gives a warning against idleness. He urges the Thessalonians to keep away from any brother or sister living irresponsibly and not in accordance with the teachings they received from him. They worked day and night, never ate without paying for it, and were not idle. The one who is unwilling to work shall not eat and there should be repercussions to those who avoid their obligation to work. They urge such people to settle down in the Lord Jesus Christ and earn the food they eat. He says to not regard these people as enemies, but just give them a warning as one would with a believer. Then he sends his final greetings and blessings to the Thessalonians. He wishes for the lord of peace himself to give them peace at all times and in every way. Paul says he writes this greeting with his own hand and wishes the grace of the Lord Jesus Christ be with them all.

1 Timothy

After Paul was released from prison in Rome, he discovered the leaders in the Ephesian church had altered the message of the gospel. This was one of the churches that Paul helped create on his missionary trips. These false leaders were mixing Jewish practices with some borrowed philosophies of the day. They were restricting certain foods, giving guidelines on marriage, and they were giving spiritual growth tips that were not aligned with the purpose or teachings of Jesus. On top of that, they were supporting immoral behavior. So, Paul sent his brother in Christ Timothy to confront Ephesus and set things in order. Timothy was a coworker and student of Paul, who he met on a missionary trip. Paul wrote him a letter that he was expected to share with the church. Paul's objective was to show what true church leadership looked like, which has Jesus as the head. He said that the source of many of their problems seems to be greed.

In chapter 1, Paul starts off by identifying himself as an apostle of the lord and introduces Timothy as his true son in faith, wishing grace, mercy, and peace from God the Father and the Lord Jesus Christ. Timothy is in charge of opposing false teachings in Ephesus and to command certain people to no longer teach false doctrines. They devote themselves to myths and endless genealogies, which only promote controversial speculations rather than advancing God's work, which is about faith. The goal of this command is love, which comes from a pure heart, a good conscience, and a sincere faith. Some have departed from these good character traits and have turned to meaningless talk. The want to be intellects and teachers of law, but they do not know what they are talking about and are confidently wrong. Paul explains that the law is good when used properly. The law is not made for the righteous ones, it was made for the lawbreakers and rebels, the ungodly and sinful, the unholy and non-religious, the ones that murder their family and all murderers, the sexually immoral, same-gender sexual acts, slave traders, liars and perjurers. It is saying that anything contrary to the sound doctrine of the true gospel is false teachings. The lord is merciful and gives grace to Paul. He was once a blasphemer, a persecutor, and a violent man. He acted in ignorance and disbelief but was shown mercy. Paul expresses his thankfulness to the Lord Jesus Christ for appointing him as a servant and for considering him trustworthy. Jesus is the source of Paul's strength, the grace of the lord was poured out on him abundantly, along with faith and love in Jesus Christ. The lord came into the world to save sinners, and Paul says he was one of the worst. This was the reason Paul was shown mercy, so Jesus could display his immense patience as an example to those who believe in him and receive eternal life. Honor and glory be forever and ever to the only God who is eternal and immortal. This chapter is a reminder of the importance of defending faith, upholding the truth of the gospel, and fighting against false teachings. Paul instructs Timothy to fight the battle defending truth, while holding on to faith and keeping a good conscience.

In chapter 2, it is a guide for prayer and worship, highlighting the essential role of Jesus Christ as a mediator. Paul urges them to pray for all people, even for kings and people of authority, so that they may live peaceful and quiet lives in all godliness and holiness. He says this is good because it pleases God, who wants people to be saved and have knowledge and truth. There is only one God and one mediator between God and mankind, and that is Jesus Christ, who gave his life as a ransom to pay for the sins of the world. Therefore, he wants all people everywhere to pray, lifting up holy hands without anger or disputing. He advises women to dress modestly, with decency and propriety, adorning themselves, but not with fancy material things like gold pearls and expensive clothes. It says that it is not permitted for a woman to assume authority over a man and should learn submission and quietness. Eve was the one who was deceived first, not Adam. Woman will be saved by Jesus Christ, as long as they continue in faith, love, and holiness.

In chapter 3, it describes the qualifications for someone who wants to be an overseer, such as being temperate, respectable, self-controlled, hospitable, able to teach, faithful to his wife, not give into drunkenness, nonviolent and gentle, not get into fights, and not obsessed with money. They cannot be a recent convert because they may become conceited and fall under the same judgement as the devil. They must also manage their family in a manner that's worthy of respect, if a man cannot take care of his own family, then how can he oversee God's church. They should also have a good reputation with those outside the church, so they do not fall into disgrace and into the devils trap. Then it describes qualifications to be a deacon, which are lower ranking clergy members of ministry. They must be worthy of respect, sincere, not indulge in much alcohol, and not pursuing dishonest gain. They must keep hold of the deep truths of the faith with a clear conscience. He says to test them out and if nothing is found against them, then let them serve as deacons. Woman must also be worthy of respect and trustworthy in everything, not malicious talkers. A deacon must be faithful to his wife and manage his household and children in a respectful manner. Those who serve well gain an excellent standing and great assurance in their faith in Christ Jesus. Paul writes the reasons for his instructions to close out chapter three. He writes so people understand how to conduct themselves in God's household, which is the church of the living God, the pillar and foundation of the truth. The mystery of godliness is about Jesus Christ and the truth about salvation and righteousness. Jesus took on human nature and became incarnate, then was vindicated by the spirit. Jesus ascended and was taken up in glory to sit at the right hand of the Father. The gospel was preached universally, the nations believed and were converted. The mystery of godliness is the fact that God took on human flesh to live among the people he created, and a believer must understand this to grow in relationship with God.

In chapter 4, Paul warns Timothy of a future time when some people will abandon the faith. They will follow deceiving spirits and things taught by demons. He says these teachings come from hypocritical liars, who have a moral conscience that is crooked. They produce rules like forbidding people to marry and abstaining from certain foods. God created all things good, and they are to be received with thanksgiving by those who believe in the truth. Things are made holy by the word of God and through prayer. It says that a good servant of Jesus Christ will point out these truths to the believers, nourished on the truths of the faith and of the good teachings that they have followed. He tells them to train themselves to be Godly and have nothing to do with godless myths and old superstitions that are not based on fact. Godliness holds value for all things, in the present and future. It says this is why they work and struggle, because they put their hope in the living God, who is the savior of all people, especially those who believe. Paul gives Timothy, who is a young preacher some lessons about the importance of personal conduct and good spiritual practice. He tells Timothy not to let anyone look down on him just because he is young, and to set an example for the believers in speech, love, in faith, and in purity. Paul says until he comes, for Timothy to devote himself to the public reading of scripture, preaching, and teaching. He says Timothy has a gift and that he should not neglect the spiritual gift God gave him, which was confirmed when the church leaders laid their hands on him. Also to be diligent in these matters and devote himself fully so others may see his progress. The last thing Paul tells

Timothy is for him to watch his life and doctrine closely, because the salvation of himself and his listeners depend on it.

In chapter 5, it discusses how believers should honor and respect widows and elderly people. It says to not rebuke an older man, treat him as if it was their own father and treat younger men as if it was their own brothers. Same with older woman, treat them as if it were their own mother and younger women as if it were their own sisters, with absolute purity. Prioritize the widows who are in the most need first, the ones who are sixty and older who do not have families taking care of them. The widows who have children and grandchildren, their kids should be taking care of them, it pleases God when children honor their parents. Anyone who does not provide for their relatives, and especially for their own household, has denied the faith and is worse than an unbeliever. The younger widow should look to remarry, rather than jumping from house to house because when they do that, they are more likely to talk nonsense and fall victim to Satan. A widow who lives only for pleasure is already dead while still living. The church had a program to take care of widows, and they needed a system to prioritize the most in need widows first. It says that elders should be worthy of extra honor, especially those who are preaching and teaching. He uses the analogy of, "Do not muzzle an ox while it is treading out the grain," meaning that people who work for the lord in ministry should be adequately compensated for their labor and deserve wages. When accusations are made against an elderly person, evidence should be gathered from multiple witnesses. Those who are sinning should be rebuked publicly, so that others may be warned. Paul emphasizes they must keep these instructions without prejudice or favoritism. Then concludes by stating that some people's sins are obvious, while others are revealed later, but nothing is hidden from God.

In chapter 6, it is a reminder to have unwavering commitment to God's commandments and staying faithful, despite all the worldly things. Those who live in accordance with God's word will receive eternal rewards. Paul addresses slaves who are believers, some were disrespecting their masters who are also believers. Paul says to remain respectful, so that God's name and their teachings may not be slandered. God is righteous and wants equality and salvation for all humans. There is nothing in the Bible that supports slavery as a morally good thing. Paul writes about false teachers and lovers of money. A human comes into this world with nothing, and they cannot take anything with them when they die. It is better to be happy and content without needing anything but food and clothing. Anyone who opposes the teachings of the Lord Jesus Christ is conceited and understand nothing. These people have an unhealthy relationship with controversies and altercations about things that only result in envy, malicious talk, evil suspicions, and paranoia. They are in constant friction with people whose minds are corrupted, who think godliness is related to financial gain. A true gain is having godliness and to be content. Those who only focus on getting rich will easily fall into temptation and desire, it is a trap that causes people to plunge into ruin and destruction. The love of money is the root of all evil, some people who were eager for money wandered from their faith and pierced themselves with many griefs. The Apostle Paul urges them to flee from all this in the world and instead pursue righteousness, godliness, faith, love, endurance, and gentleness. He says to fight the good fight of faith and take hold of eternal life. Paul says to keep this command without spot or blame until the Lord Jesus Christ's appearing, who is the king of kings and lord of lords. He says to put hope in God who provides everything, and to warn the arrogant not to put their hope in wealth which is uncertain. Be generous and willing to give and be rich in good deeds. Turn away from godless chatter and the opposing ideas of what is falsely called knowledge. Grace be with all.

2 Timothy

Second Timothy is Paul's final letter. He was facing more persecution and harm, and he was once again imprisoned in Rome. This was one of Paul's most personal letters because he expected this would be the time that the courts would find him guilty and have him executed. He writes to Timothy asking him to come to Rome. Paul ordered Alexander and Hymenaeus to step down from leadership because they were still misdirecting people into a corrupted version of faith and the gospel that focused on debate and disagreement rather than purity and respect. They continued to reject and oppose Paul. Timothy was disheartened and intimidated, but Paul pushes him to stay faithful to the true message. He warns Timothy of a time of trouble and false teachers, treacherous and insincere people. Also to remember the gospel message, which is Jesus Christ is the prophesied messiah, who came from the line of David, who was crucified and rose from the dead.

In chapter 1, it starts out acknowledging Paul as an apostle of Christ who is following the will of God, and wishing grace, mercy, and peace from God the Father and the Lord Jesus Christ. Paul remembers Timothy in his prayers and is grateful for his sincere faith, which he attributes to Timothy's grandmother Lois and his mother Eunice, who believed and instilled in Timothy his faith in the messiah. Paul calls on Timothy and believers to give their loyalty to him and the gospel. He said that God gave his spirit to the world not to cause timidness, instead for power, love, and self-discipline. He says to not be ashamed of the testimony of the lord or ashamed because he is a prisoner. He requests for Timothy to join in him suffering for the gospel, by the power of God. Jesus saves and calls them to a holy life, not because of anything they have done or because they deserve it, he saves because of grace. This grace was given in Christ before the beginning of time and has now been revealed through the appearing of the savior, Christ Jesus, who has destroyed death and brought life and immortality to light through the gospel. Paul explains his own suffering, testifying that he is not ashamed because he knows whom he has believed in and is convinced that God is able to guard what has been entrusted to him, with the help of the holy spirit that lives in them. Paul gives examples of disloyalty and loyalty. He reminded them that everyone in the province of Asia had deserted him, including Phygelus and Hermogenes, demonstrating how some people may abandon faith when facing persecution or adversity. A dedicated follower of Christ named Onesiphorus was loyal to Paul and was not ashamed of his chains, he gave unwavering support and encouragement for Paul, even during difficult times. Onesiphorus' support emphasizes the importance of remaining faithful and standing by those in need, even when others turn away.

In chapter 2, it is a call on believers to embody the virtues of a faithful servant of Christ. He says to be strong in the grace that is Jesus Christ, join with him in suffering, like a good soldier of the lord. He uses metaphors of a soldier, an athlete, and a farmer to highlight the virtues of discipline, hard work, and endurance in a believers life. All of these jobs require sacrifice and endurance to reach a greater goal. He says to reflect on this and the lord will share insight into all of this. Remember Jesus Christ who was raised from the dead and descended from David. This is the gospel, for which Paul is suffering to the point of being chained up like a criminal, but God's word can never be chained. He endures everything for the sake of the elect, so they too may obtain salvation and eternal glory through Jesus Christ. It is written that if they died with him, they will also live with him. Dying in Christ represents the act of surrendering their old life of sin and committing to follow Christ. Living with him refers to his divine promises and having a relationship with him in the present. It also says that God cannot disown or deny himself meaning that even if they are unfaithful, God remains faithful because he cannot deny his own character. This shows God's unwavering commitment to believers, regardless of their shortcomings. The next section is about dealing with false teachers. The corrupt teachings in Ephesus is spreading like an infection, and Timothy is tasked to unite them in Christ. They have distorted the teachings of the resurrection and are not teaching about how its intended purpose was for a new creation and a new humanity. He wants Timothy to appoint faithful leaders who correctly handle the word of truth and spread the good news about Jesus correctly, the message of salvation through faith in Jesus Christ. He says to avoid meaningless chatter and arguments, because those who indulge in it will become more and more ungodly. He says to flee the evil desires of youth and pursue righteousness, faith, love, and peace, along with those who call on the lord out of a pure heart. A servant of the lord must be kind to everyone and able to teach, not resentful or quick to anger. Non-believers and opposition must be instructed gently, in the hope that God will grant them repentance leading them to a knowledge of the truth. Pray for enemies and the lost, that they will come to their senses and escape from the trap of the devil, who has taken them captive to do his will.

In chapter 3, it is a warning about the terrible times in the last days. In the time of great tribulation, look for signs of society's moral decline. People will be lovers of themselves, lovers of money, proud, abusive, disobedient to their parents, ungrateful, unholy, without love, unforgiving, slanderous, without self-control, brutal, not lovers of the good, treacherous, rash, conceited, lovers of pleasure rather than lovers of God. They will have a form of godliness but deny its power, have nothing to do with such people. They are the kind of people who weasel and creep their way into the homes of gullible women, they take advantage and gain control of weak-willed women, promising relief from their guilt and are swayed by all kinds of evil desires. They are always learning but are never able to find knowledge or truth. This means they constantly seek new teachings but are never truly able to grasp the truth of faith because they are easily swayed by false teachings or their own desires, rather than seeking genuine understanding. These teachers oppose truth and their minds are depraved. They will not get very far, because their lack of morality and understanding will become clear to everyone. Paul tells Timothy that anyone who wants to live a godly life in Christ will be persecuted, while the evildoers and imposters will go from bad to worse, deceiving and being deceived. He reminds Timothy of his teachings, way of life, purpose, faith, patience, love, endurance, and the persecutions and sufferings he endured. Paul says that the lord rescued him and tells Timothy to keep going and continue in what he has learned. He encourages Timothy to remain steadfast in the truths he has learned from the scriptures, which are God-breathed and fully equipped to guide him in righteous living and every good work. He says the scriptures are useful for teaching, rebuking, correcting, and is able to give wisdom and salvation through faith in Jesus.

In chapter 4, Paul gives final instructions to Timothy, to be steadfast in faith and preach the word of God. In the presence of God and Jesus, who will judge the living and the dead, he gives Timothy this one command and that is to preach the gospel. Also to be prepared to spread the truth of the gospel in any season with great patience and careful instruction, correcting, rebuking, and encouraging. There will come a time when people do not put up with sound doctrine, they will gather around people who teach things they want to hear that suits their own desires. They seek teachers who confirm their own bias and preexisting beliefs. It describes people who reject the truth and instead embrace falsehoods and myths. He says to keep a clear head in all situations, do the work of an evangelist spreading the good news of salvation, and to complete all the duties and responsibilities entrusted in him as a minister. Paul is aware that his time on earth is coming to an end and is happy that he fought the good fight, finished the race, and kept his faith. The crown of righteousness is a metaphor representing a reward for living righteously and faithfully, which many who have longed for Jesus' appearance will receive on the day of judgement. Paul finishes out the letter with regard to some personal matters. He asks Timothy to do his best to see him quickly before he is executed. Most of his other ministry partners are away from him except Luke. Paul warns Timothy to watch out for certain people, like Alexander the metalworker, because they either oppose their message or they love the world too much. Despite everyone's desertion, the lord stood at Paul's side and strengthened him, so that through him the message could be fully proclaimed, and all the gentiles could hear it. Paul eagerly looks forward to joining Jesus in his kingdom after death, who rescues him from every evil attack, and says to him be glory for ever and ever. He wishes the lord to be with their spirit and grace be with them all.

Titus

Paul had sent Titus, a long-time co-worker with the task of going to the island of Crete to act as a representative to restore order. The message of Titus is that knowledge of truth leads to godliness, and that the grace of God offers salvation to all people.

In chapter 1, it starts out with Paul referring to Titus as his true son in their common faith, wishing grace and peace from God the Father and the Lord Jesus Christ. He says God gave a divine promise of a savior and God does not lie or ever break a promise, and that season has come. Titus is tasked to appoint elders who love what is good and follow the will of God's principles. He outlines qualifications for these overseers of God's household such as being blameless, faithful to spouse, and their kids cannot be wild or disobedient non-believers. They must not be overbearing, quick tempered, drunkards, violent, and must not be pursuing dishonest gain. Rather, they must be hospitable, love what is good, self-controlled, upright, holy and disciplined. They must truly believe in their hearts the teachings of Jesus, so that they are capable of encouraging others or capable of refuting false teachings and opposition. It says how to rebuke those who fail to do good. There are many rebellious people, full of meaningless talk and deception. They must be silenced because they are disrupting households by teaching things they should not be, usually for the sake of dishonest gain. Paul warns Titus about false teachers who are leading people astray, he says to rebuke them sharply, so they might be sound in the faith, not paying attention to Jewish myths or human commands. To the people who are pure, all things are pure, but the non-believers who are corrupted, nothing is pure, and both their minds and consciences are corrupted. They claim to know God, but their actions say otherwise denying him. They are detestable, disobedient, and unfit for anything good.

In chapter 2, it is about doing good for the sake of the gospel and teaching what is appropriate to sound doctrine. He provides specific instructions for older men, older women, young women, young men. For older men, it says to be temperate, worthy of respect, self-controlled, sound in faith, in love and endurance. For older women, it says to be reverent and respectful in the way they live, do not slander and gossip, do not be addicted to too much wine, also to teach what is good. They should urge younger women to love their husbands and children, they should be self-controlled and pure, keep themselves busy at home, and be kind. Similarly, young men should be encouraged to be self-controlled. Set an example to them by doing what is good, and when teaching, show integrity, seriousness, and soundness in speech that cannot be condemned. Opposition will be ashamed because when someone leads by example, no one can say anything bad about them, making the teachings of God more attractive to others. The grace of God appeared so that salvation may be available to all people. It teaches them to say no to ungodliness and worldly passions, to live a life that is upright, self-controlled, and godly while awaiting the glory of God the Father and the savior Jesus Christ. He gave his life to redeem humanity from all wickedness and free believers from sin. He says these are the things that should be taught, and to encourage and rebuke with all authority.

In chapter 3, it is a reminder of God's grace and his transformative power. It says believers should respect and follow the laws of their governments while actively seeking opportunities to do good deeds for others in their community. Do not slander anyone, be peaceful and considerate, and always be gentle toward everyone. He contrasts the sins of the past with the righteous living that believers should pursue. They were foolish and enslaved by all kinds of passions and pleasure, they lived in malice and envy, disobedient, and hated one another. But when the kindness and love of God the savior appeared, he saved them, not because of righteous things people had done, he saved them because of his mercy. Salvation is a gift of God's grace and mercy, resulting in a spiritual rebirth and renewal by the holy spirit, which was poured out generously through Jesus Christ. Believers have been justified by his grace and become heirs of eternal life through faith in him. Paul stresses these things to Titus so that those who trust in God can devote themselves to doing good, which is beneficial for everyone. He says that arguments over mosaic law, family genealogies, and bickering over meaningless stuff is useless and beneficial to no one. Warn divisive people once and also a second time, if they do not change, have nothing to do with them. They are warped and sinful, only condemning themselves. He says their people must learn to devote themselves to doing good in order to provide for people with urgent needs, so that their lives are not unproductive and unfruitful. He sends his final remarks and greeting, wishing grace to all.

Philemon

Paul wrote this letter from prison to Philemon, a prosperous Christian living in Colossae. Onesimus is a runaway slave of Philemon, and Paul sends this letter to Philemon as a plea to welcome him back not as a slave, but a brother in Christ. It is an example of how someone's status in life does not define their value in the kingdom of God. As believers, they are all brothers and sisters in Christ and are all equal in the eyes of God and believers should strongly encourage equality and freedom in Christ. It is a testament of the transformative power of faith, love, and forgiveness. The letter begins with Paul and Timothy sending greetings to Philemon, Apphia, Archippus, and the church in their home, wishing grace and peace from God the Father and the Lord Jesus Christ. Paul says he remembers Philemon in his prayers and always thanks God, he hears about his love and faith towards Jesus and all his holy people. He prays that their partnership with each other in faith may be effective in deepening understanding of all good things they share in Christ. His love has given Paul great joy and encouragement because he has refreshed the hearts of the lord's people.

It appeared that Onesimus, the runaway slave had stolen from Philemon on his way out. Paul makes a plea for Onesimus to be forgiven and freed, asking Philemon to show the same love and forgiveness that God had shown him. Paul says he could be bold and order that Philemon does the right thing but prefers to ask him nicely, so he willingly does it on the basis of love. He says it is none other than Paul, a prisoner in chains for Christ and in chains for the gospel who is making an appeal for his son Onesimus. He tells Philemon that Onesimus is dear to his heart and has become useful for everyone. Paul is sending Onesimus back to Philemon, requesting that he is welcomed back not as a slave, but as a fellow man and as a dear brother in the lord. Paul tells Philemon that if he respects him as a partner, then he should welcome Onesimus as he would for him. Also Paul said that if Onesimus has done Philemon wrong or owes him money, charge it to Paul himself, and he will pay it back. Paul suggests that Philemon should consider himself indebted to him spiritually, and that this debt should be greater than any material debt Onesimus owes. Paul sends his final greetings wishing the grace of the Lord Jesus Christ to be with their spirit.

Hebrews

The book of Hebrews target audience suggests it was written for Jesus believing Jews who needed a boost in their faith. There are a lot of references to the old testament, so it takes time to interpret these writings. The people who received these writings needed it because they were facing heavy persecution due to their faith in Jesus, which caused them to abandon or walk away from faith. The setting is likely around Italy. The letter recalls the first five books and the prophets from the old testament, then exalts Jesus above all of them. It compares the old covenant with the superiority of the new covenant. Jesus is a more effective teacher than the priests appointed by the laws of Moses. Jesus and salvation are greater than angels and laws from the past. Jesus brings greater peace over Moses and Joshua bringing Israel into the promised land. They are encouraged to live in the light of God's glory.

In chapter 1, it starts out by saying that Jesus Christ is God's final word and ultimate revelation. In the past God spoke to their ancestors through prophets many times in various ways, but now he speaks to them through his son who was appointed heir of all things, and the creator of all things in the universe. The son is a reflection of God's glory and an exact representation of his being. He sustains all things by his powerful word and provided purification for sins, so he became superior to angels. Jesus is different and superior to all the other angels. All the prophets were messengers of God, but Jesus is the ultimate message and truth. It states that God never addressed any other angels as "my son" or told any other angels "I will be the Father, and he will be the Son." Angels act as servants and do not have sovereign rule or act outside of Gods will. Jesus is unique in power and equal to God; he is the full and final revelation to mankind. Psalm forty-five six is referenced to show that the messiah has an everlasting throne and godly authority, all beings and angels serve the king of kings. The incarnation is a divine mystery where Jesus, who is divine, took on a lower position than the angels to fully experience and fulfill God's plan of redemption. Jesus Christ is exalted above all others because his divine nature is perfect compared to any other being, he loves righteousness and hates wickedness. Jesus was there when the foundation of earth were laid, showing his supreme authority over all creation. Humans and this world will perish but God's word and kingdom remains. Jesus is eternal and unchanging; his enemies will become nothing and in the end Jesus will have final and complete victory. The angels who work for the will of God will help support the spirits of believers toward ultimate deliverance, who are heirs of salvation.

In chapter 2, it is a warning to believers not to drift away from the faith and pay attention. The world has been given the greatest gift of salvation and the holy spirit, testified by God. It says to pay careful attention and not be too consumed by the world because it can cause someone to drift away from the lord, instead embrace the love and grace which was first announced by the lord and confirmed by those who heard him. This section emphasizes the humanity of Jesus, who was made fully human, to restore the rights of humans to rule over earth and share in his sufferings. These things were not done for angels, but for the sake of humanity. Jesus was temporarily made lower than angels for a little while, where he was crowned with glory and honor because he suffered death, so that by the grace of God he might taste death for everyone. Jesus is the pioneer of salvation, made perfect through his sufferings. They are all now brothers and sisters of the same holy family. The power of death and the devil has been broken, and the holy family of believers has been freed from their fear of death. It was a necessity for Jesus to made fully human in every way so he could make atonement for the sins of the people, becoming a merciful and faithful high priest. Jesus himself suffered and was tempted, so that he may be able to help those who are also tempted.

In chapter 3, it tells how Jesus is superior to Moses and gives a warning against unbelief. It says Jesus was faithful to the one who appointed him, just as Moses was faithful in God's house. Jesus has been found worthy of greater honor than Moses, just as the builder of a house has greater honor than the house itself. Every house was built by someone, but God is the builder of everything. Moses was a faithful servant and a testimony of what was to come, but Jesus Christ is faithful as the son over God's house. It says they are his house, as long as they firmly hold confidence and hope of glory until the end. The next part gives a warning against unbelief. The holy spirit says if someone hears his voice, do not harden the heart as they did during the rebellion in the wilderness. Their ancestors tested and tried God and for forty years, they saw what he did. That is why God was angry with that generation, because their hearts went astray and have not known his ways. It says to see to it that no one should have a sinful heart that turns away from the living God. Encourage one another daily and watch out to not be hardened by sins deceitfulness. Come together in Christ and hold conviction firmly until the very end. Believers who fail to trust in God risk losing their spiritual blessings. Israelites wandered the desert for forty years because they were faithless, this is a warning to not lose faith in the lord and salvation.

In chapter 4, it uses the term "they shall never enter my rest" referring to people who do not believe in God and therefore cannot enter his rest. It says to be careful to not fall short of God's salvation. They have received the gospel, and the good news is proclaimed to them, just as them in the wilderness heard God's calling, but did not answer or share the faith. The word of God is alive and active. It is sharper than any double-edged sword, it penetrates the soul and spirit, joints and marrow; it judges the thoughts and attitudes of the heart. Nothing in all of creation is hidden from God's sight. Everything is uncovered and laid bare before him, to which everyone must account for. Therefore, make every effort to enter that rest, so that no one will perish by following the example of disobedience and rebellion. Hold firmly to the faith professed, the faith in the high priest Jesus Christ, the Son of God who ascended into heaven. Jesus is capable of empathizing with someone's weaknesses, he was tempted just as humans are but did not sin. It says to approach God's throne of grace with confidence, so that mercy and grace may be given in time of need.

In chapter 5, it talks about requirements of being a high priest, then compares it to the ultimate high priest Jesus. High priests are selected and appointed to represent the people in matters related to God, to offer gifts and sacrifices for sins. They can deal gently with those who are ignorant and led astray since they themselves are subject to weakness. No one takes this honor on their own, but they receive it when called by God, just as Aaron was. Christ did not glorify himself to become a high priest, he was appointed by God, who declared him as his son. Jesus experienced human suffering, learned obedience, was made perfect, and became the source of eternal salvation for all who obey him. A mysterious high priest figure named Melchizedek is used to represent Jesus as the mediator between God and humans. The last section of the chapter is a warning about spiritual immaturity and the importance of growing in faith. The author compares unexperienced believers to infants who need milk instead of solid food, who are not yet acquainted with the teachings of righteousness. The solid food is for the mature, they have become stronger in understanding and with constant training of the word. These people can more easily distinguish good from evil.

In chapter 6, it urges believers to move beyond the elementary teachings about Christ and to advance in faith and understanding. It is about repentance and the consequences of falling away from God. It addresses those who have fallen away after tasting the goodness of the word of God and experienced the holy spirit. Those who have fallen away after experiencing the spirit are being brought back to repentance and crucifying the Son of God all over again and subjecting him to public disgrace. When it says "a taste" it represents those who have come so close to the truth, but easily slip away because they never fully reached salvation in the first place. It is impossible for someone who has been enlightened and saved to lose that. God's nature is unchanging, and this chapter highlights his faithfulness and covenant promises. It reassures believers the certainty of God's promises and the hope that is set. This hope is like an anchor, firm and secure. The hope in Jesus is the anchor in someone's soul, and it enters the inner sanctuary behind the curtain. The hope in Christ is steadfast and deeply rooted, providing a firm foundation in someone's heart. It is impossible for God to lie and the promise to Abraham was fulfilled because of his faith. God is just and will not forget the work and love someone shows to his people. It says to not become lazy, those with faith and patience will inherit that promise.

In chapter 7, it describes Jesus as the high priest, and it describes the unchanging nature of God's divine promises. The author goes into detail about the priesthood of Melchizedek, who was there with Abraham. Unlike other Levitical priests, Jesus' priesthood is eternal, and Christ is the ultimate and perfect fulfillment of God's promises. The new covenant with Jesus is superior to the old covenant of Levitical law. This letter was intended for persecuted Jewish Christians, and it is vital for those still trying to live under the law to understand this. Melchizedek is referenced to describe the ministry of Jesus Christ. The Old Testament separated the line of kings from the line of priests, Melchizedek held both titles. In genesis chapter fourteen section eight, Melchizedek the king of Salem brought bread and wine. He was the priest of the most high and blessed Abram saying, "blessed be Abram by the most high, the creator of heaven and earth and praise be to God Most High, who delivered your enemies into your hand." Then Abram gave him a tenth of everything. Melchizedek is superior to Abraham, Aaronic priests or Levitical priests. Jesus lives forever and had permanent priesthood, therefore is able to save those who come to God through him, because he always lives to intercede for them. The son was appointed and came after the law, who has been made perfect forever.

In chapter 8, it is a message of renewal in Jesus and the new covenant. The new covenant offers a more personal relationship with God and says he will put his laws in their minds and write it on their hearts. He will be their God, and they will be his people. He will forgive their wickedness and will remember their sins no more. By calling this covenant new, he has made the first one obsolete; and what is obsolete and outdated will soon disappear.

In chapter 9, it shows the transformative shift from the old covenant to the new. It conveys the redemptive power of Christ and the significance of the new covenant. His blood shed was the perfect sacrifice obtaining eternal redemption. His blood cleanses consciences from dead works. Christ has always been God's ultimate plan for salvation. The blood of Christ, through the eternal spirit offered himself unblemished to God to cleanse consciences from acts that lead to death, so that they may serve the living God. For this reason, Christ is the mediator of a new covenant, those who are called may receive the promised eternal inheritance. He has died as a ransom to set them free from the sins committed under the first covenant. The law requires that nearly everything be cleansed with blood, and without the shedding of blood there is no forgiveness. Christ would have had to suffer many times since the creation of the world; he only had to appear once for all of the ages to do away with sin by the sacrifice of himself. Just as people are destined to die once, and after that to face judgment. Christ was sacrificed once to take away the sins of many. He will appear a second time, not to bear sin, but to bring salvation to those who are waiting for him.

In chapter 10, it details Christ's sacrifice on the cross as the atonement for sins. The law and old covenant was a reminder of sin and a mirror revealing sin, not a removal of them. Its intended purpose was a shadow of the good things to come, not the realities themselves. Sacrifices were performed annually; these rituals only served as reminders of sins instead of eliminating them. It is impossible for the blood of animals to take away sins. Therefore, Christ came into the world and was made holy through the sacrifice of his body, once for all. Day after day priests would perform religious duties; again and again they offers the same sacrifices, which can never take away sins. When Jesus came, he had offered a one-time sacrifice for the sins of the world and sat down at the right hand of God. By that one sacrifice, he has been made perfect and holy forever, and the holy spirit testifies to that. The lord says this is the new covenant, and will put it in their minds and write it in their hearts. God offers complete forgiveness to humanity in the new covenant, and sacrifice for sin is no longer necessary.

Believers are called to persevere in faith and enter the most holy place with confidence because a new way a living has opened up through the blood of Jesus. It says to help one another toward love and good deeds, and to draw near to God with a sincere heart with the full assurance that faith brings, having the hearts cleansed from a guilty conscience and having bodies washed with pure water. It says to hold onto that hope professed all the more as you see the day of the lord approaching. The author gives a warning to those who deliberately keep sinning after receiving the truth of knowledge because there will be a day of judgement. Some may interpret this in different ways, but it refers to apostasy, or abandoning faith, just as those in the wilderness did. It is insult to the spirit of grace to turn ones back on the Son of God after receiving the blood of the covenant that sanctified them. The lord will judge his people, and it is a dreadful thing to fall into the hands of the living God. It reminds them of all the persecution and insults they had to endure. It reminds them of the times they had all their possessions confiscated and put in jail, and they joyfully accepted it because they knew they had better and lasting possessions in the next life. So it says to not throw away their confidence in the lord, because it will be richly rewarded. It encourages them to persevere in doing God's will because if they do, they will receive what he has promised. Those who have faith in the lord will be saved and those who turn their backs on faith will be destroyed. The righteous ones live by faith, and he who is coming will come soon.

In chapter 11, it is about the importance of faith and putting it into action. God's perfect and divine plan will unfold in his timing, and it is impossible to please God without faith. Faith is about maintaining hope and assurance in God's promises. This chapter lists old testament figures who had faith such as Abel, Enoch, Jacob, Noah, Abraham and Moses. By faith it is understood that the universe was formed at God's command. Moses chose to be mistreated along with the people of God rather than to enjoy the fleeting pleasures of sin, because he had faith in God. Moses saw greater value in God the Father over the treasures of Egypt, because he was looking ahead to his reward. Noah could not see the future and was warned about things that are not seen, but he still built the ark and became an heir to righteousness. Abraham was called to go to a foreign place he did not know or how he would receive his inheritance, but he made his home in tents and trusted the lord. All these people were still living in faith when they died. They could not see the future and how God's plan unfolded thousands of years later, they only saw them and welcomed them from a distance. By faith, the walls of Jericho fell, after the army had marched around them for seven days. Gideon, Barak, Samson, Jephthah, David, Samuel, and the prophets conquered kingdoms through faith, administered justice, and gained what was promised. They were all commended for their faith, yet none of them received what had been promised. God had planned something better for all of humanity so that only together they would be made perfect.

In chapter 12, it urges believers to run the race of faith with perseverance. God wants them to examine sin in their life and ask him for a way out, focusing on Jesus who is the pioneer and perfecter of faith. It says to remember Jesus and the opposition he received from sinners, so that they do not grow weary and lose heart. The next section describes God like a parent who disciplines his children. Enduring struggles and hardships is a form a heavenly discipline and God disciplines the ones he loves, just as an earthly parent would. They all had human fathers who disciplined them and respected them for it. They disciplined their kids for a little while as they thought best; but God disciplines them for their own good, so they may share in his holiness. It says to make every effort to live in peace with everyone and to be holy, because without holiness no one will see the lord. Warn others so that no one falls short of God's grace and that no bitter root grows to cause trouble and defile many. The author contrasts the mountain of fear at Mount Sinai with the mountain of joy which is the heavenly Mount Zion. Jesus the mediator of a new covenant and believers are part of this joyful assembly. Do not reject the voice of God, his voice shook the earth before and will do so again. God's kingdom is unshakable, so be thankful always and worship him with reverence.

In chapter 13, it is the last chapter encouraging believers to conduct and apply Christ in their lives. Love one another as brothers and sisters. Show hospitality to strangers because some people have interacted with angels without even realizing. Every act of kindness carries the potential for divine significance. It says to empathize with those who are in prison as if they were with them in prison, and to empathize with those who are mistreated as if they are the ones suffering. Keep marriages honorable and pure, for God will judge the adulterer and all the sexually immoral. The author tells them to be content with what they already have, and keep their lives free from the love of money, because God says he will never leave or forsake them. The passage quotes the Psalms about trusting in the lord, declaring that they should not fear what man can do to them. Do not be led astray by all kinds of strange teachings and remember the true leaders of faith are the ones who speak the word of God. It is good for their hearts to be strengthened by grace. Jesus is the same yesterday, and today, and forever. Believers are reminded that they do not belong to this world and should seek the heavenly city that is to come. They are encouraged to do good deeds and praise God as a form of sacrifice to please him. Also, to have a clear conscience and to live honorably. The chapter concludes with a prayer and finals greetings. May the God of peace, who through the blood of the eternal covenant was brought back from the dead, Lord Jesus equip them with everything good for doing his will. Grace be with all and may he work in believers to do what is pleasing to God through Jesus Christ, to whom be glory for ever and ever.

James

James was one of the brothers of Jesus, he became a church leader in Jerusalem after Jesus' death and resurrection. Most of the believers there were Jewish people who followed Jesus. He wrote down some of his teachings, advice, and short sayings, sending his words to believers scattered around the Roman empire. It offers practical wisdom like perception of money, how to speak properly, purity, community, understanding temptations, patience, and endurance during times of trial. It inspires believers to embrace struggle and hardships as a means of building character and living out faith through compassion for others. The wisdom remains valuable for all ages and all generations.

In chapter 1, it starts out with James, who is a servant of God and the Lord Jesus Christ greeting the twelve tribes who are scattered among the nations. He says whenever they face trials, consider it pure joy because the testing of their faith produces perseverance. It says perseverance must do its work so they can become pure and complete, not lacking in anything. If anyone lacks wisdom, they should ask God because he gives generously without finding fault. It will be given as long as they believe and do not have doubt, because the one who doubts is like a wave in the sea, blown and tossed by the wind. The person who doubts should not expect anything from the lord. Such a person is double-minded and unstable in all they do. Believers should take pride in their elevated spiritual position because true worth is not found in how much material wealth a person can acquire. Their wealth will pass away like a wildflower and true worth is found through faith and spiritual growth. Blessed are the ones who persevere under trials, they will receive the crown of life that the lord has promised to those who love him. James clarifies that nobody should use the phrase "God is tempting me" because God cannot be tempted by evil, nor does he tempt anyone. Each person that is tempted is dragged away and enticed by their own evil desire. Once that desire is conceived, it gives birth to sin, and when sin is grown it gives birth to death. Every good and perfect gift comes from God who does not change like shifting shadows. God chose to give humans birth through the word of truth, so they would be the first fruits of all he created.

Everyone should be quick to listen, slow to speak and slow to become angry. Human anger does not produce the righteousness that God desires. Humbly accept the word of truth that has been planted because it saves, therefore get rid of all the moral filth and evil that is so prevalent. Do not just listen to the word, apply it. Anyone who listens to the word but does not do what it says is like someone who looks at his face in a mirror, and after looking at himself, goes away and immediately forgets what he looks like. Blessed are those who looks intently into the perfect law that gives freedom and applies it to their life, and not forgetting what they heard. Those who consider themselves religious or spiritual but do not keep their mouth in check are only deceiving themselves, their religion is worthless. A person should try their best not to be polluted by the things of the world and look after orphans and widows who are in distress. This is pure and faultless religion that God the Father accepts.

In chapter 2, it demonstrates how a person's faith should manifest through their actions. James says believers in the Lord Jesus Christ must not to show favoritism. If a wealthy man comes to a gathering wearing fancy clothes and a poor man with filthy clothes also comes to that gathering, and the wealthy one gets offered a seat and the poor man does not, then they have discriminated among themselves and become judges with evil thoughts. God has already chosen the rich in faith to inherit the kingdom he promised to those who love him. It is often the rich who are exploiting people, dragging them to court, dishonoring the poor, and blaspheming the noble name of Jesus. The royal law found in scripture is to love your neighbor as yourself, and if anyone shows favoritism that is a sin, they are convicted by the law as lawbreakers. Whoever keeps the whole law yet stumbles at just one point is guilty of breaking all of it. Mercy triumphs over judgment, those who show no mercy will be judged without mercy. James discusses faith and deeds, he asks if someone claims to have faith but does not act in accordance, are they really saved. Love and faith should be manifested through actions. He says to imagine a brother or sister is without clothes or food and someone walks up to them and says, "Go in peace; keep warm and well fed" offering them comforting words but do not physically do anything for them. He asks what good is that. In the same way, if faith by itself is not accompanied by action, it is dead. Genuine faith results in participation of good works. Just believing that there is one God or stating that God is real is not enough, even the demons believe that. Real faith is putting complete trust and obedience in God, just as Abraham did offering his son at the altar. His faith and actions were working together; his faith was considered righteous and made complete by what he did. Same with Rahab, the Canaanite prostitute who helped the Israelite spies escape Jericho, showing both faith and obedience. As the body without the spirit is dead, faith without deeds is dead.

    In chapter 3, it calls for believers to reflect on the words they speak and the significance of godly wisdom. James says that many of them should not become teachers because those who teach will be judged more strictly. Anyone who keeps their mouth and what they say in check, they are able to keep the rest of their body in check. He compares the tongue to a small bit that controls a horse or a small rudder that steers a large ship, they are small parts that power the larger whole. He also compares the tongue to fire; a great forest fire is usually started by a small spark. Likewise a person's tongue can set their whole life on fire and corrupt their whole body. All kinds of animals, birds, reptiles, and sea creatures have been tamed by mankind, but no human being can tame the tongue. It is a restless evil, full of deadly poison. The tongue is capable of both worship and harm, it can be used to praise the lord, or it can be used to curse at other human beings who were made in God's likeness. It is inconsistent and dishonorable for the same mouth to curse and praise, this should not be. Fresh water and salt water cannot flow from the same spring and fig trees cannot grow olives; he uses these comparisons to show that the mouth should only be used for praise. James says there are two kinds of wisdom, earthly wisdom which is unspiritual and demonic, verses heavenly wisdom from above which is pure, peace-loving, considerate, submissive, full of mercy, impartial, and sincere. Earthly wisdom harbors bitterness, envy, and selfish ambition in the heart. Wherever there is envy and selfish ambition, they will find disorder and every evil practice. These two types of wisdoms will manifest in people's lives and can be seen in their actions and deeds. Peacemakers who sow in peace will reap a harvest of righteousness.

    In chapter 4, it is about submitting to God and overcoming internal conflict. He acknowledges that fights and arguments stem from battles and desires within themselves. When they do not get the things they desire, they fight and kill, the reason they do not have the things they want is because they have not asked God genuinely. Sometimes people do not get what they want because their intent and motives are wrong, and God knows they would just spend it on selfish pleasures. James warns against friendship with the world, which he equates with enmity against God. Anyone who chooses to love the world becomes an enemy of God. He quotes a proverb about God longing for the spirit he intended to dwell in humanity, which is why he gives grace, and it says God opposes the proud but shows favor to the humble. Submit to God and resist the devil and he will flee. Drawing near to God will result in God drawing near to them. He urges them to cleanse their hands and purify their hearts, to grieve, mourn, and wail for their sins, and to humble themselves before the lord so that he can lift them up. James cautions against speaking ill of one another, emphasizing that those who judge their brothers and sisters are essentially speaking against the law and judging it. He reminds them that there is only one lawgiver and judge who is able to save and destroy, and they should not take on that role themselves. James writes about people who boast about their future. Some people will be like tomorrow we will go to this city or that city, spend a year here or there, carry on business and make some money there. He says people do not even know if tomorrow is guaranteed or what will happen, what is anyone's life but a mist that appears for a little while and then vanishes. Instead they should phrase it by saying "If it is the lord's will, we will live and do this or that." All forms of boasting is evil, like the arrogant schemes they plan. If anyone knows what is right and knows what they should be doing and does not, that is a sin.

In chapter 5, it is a warning to the rich oppressors who have hoarded wealth in the last days, condemning them for their exploitation of workers and their self-indulgence. The workers have cried out against the oppressors for wages they failed to pay them, these cries have reached the ears of the Lord Almighty. He encourages believers to be patient and stand firm until the lord's coming. He stresses the importance of not grumbling against one another, so that they do not fall under judgment. The lord is full of compassion and mercy, blessed are the ones who have persevered with patience in the face of suffering, as shown with prophets like Job. The chapter ends with a prayer of faith. It says that if one of them should wander from the truth and someone should bring that person back, remember this, whoever turns a sinner from the error of their way, they will save them from death and cover over a multitude of sins. He says to pray for one another and lift each other up so they may be healed, the prayer offered in faith will make the sick person well; the lord will raise them up. If they have sinned, they will be forgiven.

1 Peter

Peter Simon is the same disciple that Jesus appointed. He played a large missionary role in Jerusalem, then he spent the final years of his life as a leader in the church in Rome. When he heard of other churches being persecuted, he wrote to them urging them to remain faithful to Jesus. This letter emphasizes a message of hope and shows the new life they have in Jesus. Their trials and hardships have purpose, although it is painful, it is refining their faith in their spiritual growth as well as bringing glory to Christ.

In chapter 1, it starts out with Peter addressing the believers scattered throughout the provinces. They have been chosen according to the foreknowledge of God the Father, through the sanctifying work of the spirit, to be obedient to Jesus Christ and sprinkled with his blood. He wishes grace and peace to them. He praises God the Father and the Lord Jesus Christ, because of his grace, they have been given new birth through living hope provided by the resurrection of Jesus Christ. He refers to an imperishable inheritance kept in heaven for believers. They are shielded by God's power because of their faith until the coming salvation revealed in the last time. Peter emphasizes the importance of faith during trials, comparing their faith to gold that is refined by fire. Though they have not seen Jesus, they love him and believe in him, and they are filled with an inexpressible and glorious joy. Although the may have grief now because of the suffering, their genuine faith will be rewarded with the salvation of their souls. He encourages them to be holy and prepare their minds, be alert and sober setting their hope fully on the grace to be given when Jesus Christ is revealed. It says not to conform to the evil desires of the flesh that they once did when living in ignorance. Be holy because God is holy, the father judges each person's work impartially. He told them to live their lives on earth like foreigners in reverent fear because they were sanctified by the precious blood of Christ, not by perishable material things. He was chosen before the world was even created but was revealed in these last times for humanity's sake. Love one another deeply from the heart. They have been purified and born again though the living and enduring word of God.

In chapter 2, it starts out with Peter telling believers to rid themselves of all malice and all deceit, hypocrisy, envy, and slander of every kind. It says to crave pure spiritual milk like newborns so they may grow in salvation and faith. He uses a metaphor of a house where believers are stones and Jesus is the corner stone. Peter gives advice on living life as a follower of Jesus in an ungodly society like pagan society. He encourages them to live such good lives so that when someone accuses them of doing wrong, they may see their good deeds and glorify God on the day he visits. They are a chosen people, a royal priesthood, a holy nation, God's special possession. He says to abstain from evil desires because it is only wages war against a person's own soul. Doing good actions will silence the ignorant talk of foolish people. Show proper respect to everyone, love the family of believers, fear God, and honor the authority for the lord's sake. He told them if they are beaten while doing good things, this is commendable before God because Christ suffered when doing good. He did not make threats or retaliate; he entrusted himself to him who judges justly. It is commendable to take unjust suffering without complaint because that means they are conscious of God. Jesus bore the sins on the cross, so that the world might die to sins and live for righteousness. It says in Isaiah, "by his wounds we are healed."

In chapter 3, it discusses duties for wives and husbands for harmonious relationships, unity, and suffering. Wives are called to submit to their husbands, some men may not believe the word and may be won over by the behavior of their wives. When they see their wives acting with purity and reverence, they can be drawn to God without even using words because of their wives actions. Their beauty should not come from material outside appearance, rather it should be within their inner self. The most beautiful thing is the unfading beauty of a gentle, kind, and quiet spirit, which has great worth in God's sight. Even Sarah used to call Abraham her lord. Husbands have a duty to be considerate in the way they live with their wives and treat them with respect. Then Peter gives some advice on living righteously. He says to be like minded, be sympathetic, love one another, be compassionate and humble. He discourages retaliation like repaying evil with evil or insult with insult. Instead, repay evil with blessing, so that they may inherit a blessing. For those who seek to love life and see good days must keep their tongue from evil and their lips from deceitful speech. They must turn from evil and do good. They must seek peace and pursue it. The eyes of the lord are watching the righteous and his ears are attentive to their prayers, but the lord's back is turned to those who do evil. Even if someone suffers for doing good and what is right, they are still blessed, do not fear threats or be frightened. Always be prepared to answer anyone who asks the reasons for having hope with gentleness and respect and revering Christ as lord in the heart. Keep a clear conscience, so those who speak maliciously against good behavior will be embarrassed by their own slander. If it is God's will, it is better to suffer for doing good than turning to evil. Christ had to suffer for sins to bring humans closer to God. He was put to death in body but made alive in spirit. Christ, who has gone into heaven and is at the right hand of God, is the ultimate authority over all creation, angels, and everything that is.

In chapter 4, it is about living for God. It calls for believers to embrace suffering and to be ready for Christ's return. Peter says for them to live for God and to arm themselves with the same mindset as Christ, who suffered in the flesh. As a result, believers should live their earthly lives for the will of God and not for evil human desires. Peter lets them know that they will feel pressure and judgement from those living in sin for not participating in their reckless and wild living. They live in debauchery, lust, drunkenness, orgies, carousing, and detestable idolatry. All will have to account to God who is ready to judge the living and dead. The end of all things is near, so be alert and of sober mind to pray. Above all, love each other deeply, because love covers a multitude of sins. Offer hospitality to one another without complaining. Believers receive gifts and skills differently in the body of Christ, use that to serve others as faithful stewards of God's grace in its various forms. When speaking or serving, it should be done in the glory of God. He says to be prepared to suffer as a follower of Christ. He says to not act surprised when something strange happens or if a fiery ordeal pops up in life as a test. Always be rejoicing when participating in the sufferings of Christ, they will be overjoyed when his glory is revealed. If someone feels insulted when they hear Jesus' name being insulted, that means they are blessed and the spirit of glory and God rests in them. He says if they have suffer for believing in Jesus, do not be ashamed, but praise God. Those who suffer according to God's will should commit themselves to their faithful creator and continue to do good.

In chapter 5, it begins with Peter addressing the elders. He urges them to be shepherds of God's flock, not because they must, but because they are willing, as God wants them to be. He tells them to humble themselves under God's mighty hand, so they may be lifted up in due time. God opposes the proud and shows favor to the humble, cast anxieties to him because he is a caring God. Be alert of the enemy because the devil prowls around like a roaring lion looking for someone to devour. Stand firm in faith and resist the devil. The God of all grace restores and calls people to his eternal glory in Christ, the suffering will be no more by standing firm and having steadfast faith. It ends with him sending his final greetings, saying to greet one another with kisses of love and wish peace to all who are in Christ.

2 Peter

This letter was intended for the same audience as the previous one, and it was around sixty-five AD. Peter was imprisoned in Rome. Emperor Nero was on a Christian killing spree and Peter became aware of the fact that he would likely be found guilty and executed. As an eyewitness of Jesus and his ministry, he wrote another letter to the believers confirming the real teachings of Jesus. People were living immoral lives and spreading false teachings, much of the letter is correcting those false teachings. They were spreading misinformation saying Jesus is not returning and there is no second coming. Peter says to be patient because God wants to give as many people as possible a chance to repent, giving them more time for their souls to be saved. He says to live good lives filled with hope while looking forward to the new heaven and earth, where righteousness reigns.

In chapter 1, it starts out with Peter addressing the recipients of the letter who were first century followers of Christ, wishing them grace and peace in abundance through the acknowledgement of God the Father and the Lord Jesus Christ. He says that God's divine power has given them everything they need for a godly life through the knowledge given to them from the glorious God of goodness. God has made divine promises they can participate in to escape the corruption of this world caused by evil desires. Peter encourages believers to make every effort to develop their spiritual growth by acting on virtues such as faith, knowledge, self-control, and perseverance that leads to godliness, mutual affection, and love. Acting and growing in these measures will lead to an effective and productive life as a follower of Jesus. Whoever fails to act on these virtues will have spiritual blindness and forget that they have been cleansed from their past sins. He says to make every effort to act on their callings from God and if they do that, they will never stumble and will receive a rich welcome into the eternal kingdom of the lord. Peter writes these things because he says it is his duty as an eyewitness to the lord's glory, and to repeatedly refresh their memories of the truth. He remembers Jesus on the sacred mountain hearing the voice from heaven and witnessing the voice say, "This is my Son, whom I love; with him I am well pleased." The chapter closes out with Peter saying that the source of prophecy is always from God, interpreted by humans carried along by the spirit. Prophecy of scripture is not the prophets own interpretation of things or from human will, it is God sending wisdom through humans.

In chapter 2, Peter gives a warning against false teachers. They lead many astray with fabricated stories. They even enter churches claiming to be against heresy, yet many follow their depraved conduct, using deception to get believers to deny the sovereign lord. They disgrace truth but only bring destruction upon themselves. Believers should expect to see these false teachers, they will claim to be Christians, but their teachings contradict the message of Jesus. They are greedy and they exploit, but their judgement is imminent. For God did not spare the angels when they sinned, putting them in chains of darkness to be held for judgement. God did not spare the ancient world when he brought the flood, nor did he spare Sodom and Gomorrah when they were burnt to ashes. God will save his people and condemn the wicked on the day of judgement because he is both merciful and just. This is especially true for those who only follow the corrupt desires of the flesh, they are boldly arrogant. These false teachers are arrogantly disrespecting angels too, blaspheming on issues they know nothing about. They are creatures of instinct acting like unreasonable animals only to be caught and destroyed. They will perish and be paid back for the harm they have done; they are blots and blemishes just living in pleasure while they dine with others. They never stop sinning, full of adultery, seducing the unstable, and are experts in greed. They are out here promising freedom yet are slaves of their own depravity, for people are slaves to whatever has mastered them. They have walked off the straight way and wandered off to follow the wicked ways of Balaam, only thinking about personal gain at the expense of moral integrity. He uses the metaphor of a well without water, promising refreshment but delivering nothing. Their mouths are full of boastful words but are empty people with nothing to offer. They are appealing to lustful desires of the flesh, enticing people who are looking for an escape. The fate of those who have been liberated from Christ and turn away have dire consequences, it would have been better if they never knew Christ in the first place.

In chapter 3, it is about the day of the lord. Peter writes this second letter as a reminder to stimulate wholesome thinking. In the last days, the bitter ridiculers will come who live by their evil desires and doubt the second coming of Christ. False teachers will dispute Jesus' second coming with deceptive mocking, they will say look, earth keeps going on as it always has since creation. They will say if he were going to come he would have come by now and there will not be a day of judgement, carrying on with their sin doing whatever they want. They deliberately ignore the fact that the heavens and earth were formed from God's word, earth is from water and water has been used for destruction previously with the great flood of Noah. By this same word, the current heavens and earth are reserved for fire, being kept for the day of judgement and destruction of the ungodly. He says to not forget this one important thing, with the lord a day is like a thousand years, and a thousand years is like a day. The lord is not slow in keeping his promise, he is being patient with humans, not wanting anyone to perish and as many people to come to repentance. The day of the lord will come like a thief in the night. The heavens will disappear with a roar; the elements will be destroyed by fire, and the earth and everything in it will be laid bare. After hearing this, they are urged to live holy and godly lives as they look forward to this day, because it will come quickly and unexpectedly. On that day, the heavens will be destroyed by fire, and the elements will melt in the heat. God always fulfills his promises, and they should look forward to a new heaven and earth where righteousness dwells. Make every effort to be found spotless, blameless, and at peace with him. It is important to understand the lord's patience and its purpose because God's patience means salvation, just as Paul wrote about with the wisdom God gave him. He writes the same way in all his letters, speaking about the day of the lord. His letters contain some things that are hard to understand, which ignorant and unstable people distort, as they do the other scriptures, to their own destruction. Since they have been forewarned, he says to be on guard so they may not be carried away by lawlessness, falling from their secure position. He finishes the letter by encouraging them to grow in grace and knowledge of the lord and savior Jesus Christ. To him be glory both now and forever.

1 John

The letter called first John is a calling for believers to reflect on their lives and it describes God as an intimate God who has a personal relationship with his children. Some first century people believed they had a higher spiritual insight on God, placing themselves above other believers, which caused confusion and made them uncertain about everything they have been taught. This writing emphasizes godly living and caring for others as a sign of those who genuinely believe in God. The main points of the three Johns is about life, love, and truth.

In chapter 1, it proclaims the word of life and affirms the authenticity of Jesus Christ, who the disciples, eyewitnesses, and apostles have heard, touched, and seen with their eyes. Jesus provides eternal life through his sacrifice on the cross for the sins of the world. The Father appeared to them, and life appeared. They are sharing the importance of their personal testimonies and sharing the gospel with other believers. This proclamation is so others may have fellowship with God the Father and the Lord Jesus Christ. John states the divine nature of God, which is that he is light and in him there is no darkness. If someone claims to have a relationship with God but walks in darkness, they are lying to themselves and not living out the truth. It stresses the importance of not living in sin, if someone walks in light, then they have a relationship with God because he is light and that should reflect how they interact with other people. The blood of Jesus purifies sin. If anyone claims they are sinless, then they are deceiving themselves and the truth is not in them. If someone claims to be perfect without sin, that is essentially calling the lord a liar and the word is not in them. If they confess their sins, they will be forgiven because God is faithful and purifies people from unrighteousness.

In chapter 2, Jesus is represented as the perfect manifestation of God. God sent the holy spirit to the world so the sins of the world can be forgiven through the perfect sacrifice. This is the foundation of the holy trinity. He gives wisdom on how to decipher a true believer verses someone who claims to know him but does not. If someone disregards the commandments as irrelevant, they do not know him. People who are made complete in him obey his word and live their lives according to how Jesus did. Anyone who claims to be living in the light but hates a brother or sister is still in darkness. Anyone who loves their brother or sister lives in light and nothing can make them stumble. If someone goes around hating other people, they are living in darkness and do not know where they are going because the darkness has blinded them. He writes this so they understand that their sins have been forgiven on account of his name, and they have overcome the evil one. They already know the Father was there since the beginning, and the word of God lives in them because they are strong. He reminds them to not be part of this world because lovers of this world do not have the Father in them. All the things of this world, the lust, the desires, the lust of the eyes, and the pride of life does not come from the Father, but from the world. The world and people's desires will pass away, but whoever does the will of God lives forever.

It gives a warning against denying the son. The last hour is imminent, and the antichrist is coming. There are other forms of antichrists that have already come. These false teachers claim to be a part of Christ, but they never really belonged to him. Their teachings contradict and oppose the teachings of the word. The ones who know the truth are the anointed ones; it is impossible for them to lie when they know the truth. Whoever denies that Jesus is the messiah is an antichrist, which is separate from the antichrist of the great tribulation, they deny the Father and the son. Whoever denies the son lacks a true relationship with the Father. He is warning them so they can be aware of the people who will try to lead them astray, the lord has promised eternal life and tells them to remain faithful. The anointing they receive from God is the holy spirit, which gives them an intimate understanding of truth. The spirit that is living in them allows them to distinguish truth from fiction. God views his people as his children and is concerned for their spiritual wellbeing, emphasizing the importance of an ongoing relationship with him, so they may be confident and unashamed at his coming.

In chapter 3, it continues expressing the profound love that the Father has lavished upon believers, calling them God's children. They are set apart from the rest of the world and the world does not recognize them because they knew God. He tells them to purify themselves and live righteously as they anticipate the second coming of Jesus Christ. Those born of God do not make a practice of sinning because God's seed remains in them. The devil has been sinning and leading people astray since the beginning, the son of God appeared in order to destroy the devils work. This is how people can distinguish who the children of God are and who the children of the devil are. Anyone who does not do what is right or does not love their brothers and sisters are not of God. This is the message that has been said repeatedly, to love one another. Do not be like Cain, who belonged to evil and murdered his own brother, he did it because his brothers actions were righteous, and his actions were evil. He says to not be surprised if the world hates them because once they pass from death to life, they love each other unconditionally. Anyone who does not love remains in death. If they live their life hating one another, than they do not have eternal life residing in them. This is how they know what love is, someone who is willing to sacrifice their life for their brothers and sisters, just as Jesus laid down his life for the world. If someone has material possessions and sees a brother or sister struggling and has no pity or empathy, that person does not have the love of God in them. Love is not just about words said or speech, it is shown through actions and in truth. He encourages them to remain steadfast in their faith, keeping God's commandments and loving one another with the help of the holy spirit that lives in them.

In chapter 4, he gives on advice how to test whether spirit are from God or not. It says not to just believe anyone because many false prophets have come and are yet to come. Test them by seeing if they believe in the incarnation of Jesus as God, if they cannot acknowledge Jesus is from God than their revelation is false. They are from the world and therefore speak from the viewpoint of the world, and the world listens to them. Observe who is listening and who is not as a way to recognize the spirit of truth and the spirit of falsehood. The next part says to love one another because that love comes from God and anyone who loves God knows God. God is love, anyone who does not love, does not know God. God revealed his love by sending his one and only son into the world so that they might live through him. Jesus loved humanity so much that he paid the price for the sins of the world. Since God loved people, then it is people's duty to love one another. No one has ever seen God; but if they love one another, God lives in them, and his love is made complete in them. Through the spirit is how someone should know if God lives in them. If anyone acknowledges that Jesus is the son of God, God lives in them and they in God. Perfect love eliminates and casts out fear. If they are fearful, it implies that they are not yet fully aware of God's perfect love. Humans ability to love is only possible because of God's initial act of love. Whoever claims to love God yet hates a brother or sister is a liar. Anyone who loves God must also love their brother and sister.

In chapter 5, it offers assurance to the believers about their faith. He begins by stating that everyone who believes that Jesus is the Christ is born of God. This love for God's children is demonstrated by loving God and carrying out his commands. John emphasizes that these commands are not burdensome, for everyone born of God overcomes the world. This victory is achieved through faith, and it is their faith that enables them to overcome the world. He delves into the testimony of Jesus Christ, who came by water and blood. It is the spirit who testifies because the spirit is the truth. There are three that testify: the spirit, the water, and the blood; and these three are in agreement. They accept human testimony, but God's testimony is greater because it is the testimony of God, which he has given about his son. Whoever believes in the son of God accepts this testimony. Whoever does not believe God has made him out to be a liar, because they have not believed the testimony God has given about his son. This testimony God has given provides eternal life and this is in his son. Whoever has the son has life; whoever does not have the son of God does not have life. God hears prayers and provides anything that is asked according to his will. The chapter concludes with a warning to keep away from idols because the whole world is under the control of the evil one. The ones born of God have protection and the evil one cannot harm them. The son of God has come and revealed truth and understanding, he is the true God that offers eternal life.   (Many have authored books about verse seven and eight missing which says three bear record in heaven, the father, the word, and the spirit and those three are one.

2 and 3 John

Second John is a reminder for believers to live in truth and love. It is a warning against heresy; to be equipped with the word so they know the difference. He wishes grace and peace from God the Father and the Lord Jesus Christ. John refers to the church as a lady chosen by God and its members her children. He reminds them to not lose focus in their faith and to walk in the truth that lives in them; he was pleased to see the children walking in faith just as the Father commanded. He reminds them of the command that has been told since the beginning, to love one another. To love one another is to understand God's love. He says these things to warn them of constant deceivers and false teachers. Anyone who denies the holiness of Jesus Christ in the flesh is a deceiver and is against them. He says to not lose everything they have worked for so they may be rewarded fully. Their souls are in danger if they turn their backs on the lord because the evil one is looking for new ways to lead people astray every day. He wrote this to protect believers from evil deception, anyone who continues following the word has both the Father and the son in them. He suggests to not bring these false teachers into their homes or welcome them, so they do not fall victim to sharing in their evil work.

Third John is a letter from apostle John to Gaius, who was a devoted member of early Jesus community. He praises Gaius for his faithfulness and hospitality towards fellow believers and strangers alike. John has no greater joy than hearing believers are practicing their faith and walking in truth. It says to show hospitality to all people so they can work together for the truth. He says that a church leader named Diotrephes was turning people away, kicking out fellow believers, and spreading malicious nonsense, this is an example on what not to do as a follower of Jesus. Do not imitate evil and do what is good, God does not see people who do evil.

Jude

Jude was a half-brother to Jesus and did not play a major role but ended up being a church leader after Jesus' death. He encourages believers to stay faithful to the original message of Jesus and watch out for the people defiling the church, threatening the faith that was entrusted to God's holy people. It is a call to uphold the foundations of faith, to lean on the spirit for understanding, to understand the mercy of Jesus, and to keep God's love.

The writing starts out with him acknowledging that he is a servant to the lord, and he wishes mercy and peace in abundance in the name of God the Father and the Lord Jesus Christ. He says he was originally going to write about the salvation they share but felt compelled to warn them of the perverts who slipped their way into the church. He said these ungodly individuals are among them, they pervert the grace of the lord, using it as a license for immorality and deny Jesus as the sovereign lord. There will be judgement and consequences for ungodliness, just like the ones who stopped believing even after being delivered from slavery out of Egypt. Just like the angels who decided to exalt themselves above God, who are in chains until the great day. Just like Sodom and Gomorrah and the surrounding towns who gave themselves up to sexual immorality and perversion. They serve as an example of those who suffer the punishment of eternal fire. These ungodly people pollute their own bodies, reject authority, and heap abuse on God creations. Not even the archangel Michael had the audacity to slander or condemn God's celestial creations, when he was disputing the devil he just told him, "The Lord rebuke you!" Yet these people slander and talk about things they know nothing about. These people are blemishes who are bold and arrogant, they only live to feed themselves. He describes their behavior in vivid detail, quoting Enoch's prophecy of God's coming judgment on the ungodly. Jude calls on followers of Jesus to remain steadfast in their faith, encouraging them to keep themselves in God's love as they wait for the mercy of the Lord Jesus Christ to bring them to eternal life. They have been forewarned multiple times about the scoffers who only follow their ungodly desires following mere instincts, they do not have the spirit and divide people. It says to be merciful and empathetic to the doubters, their souls can still be saved, snatching them from the fires of this corrupted earth. Show them mercy as God shows mercy, hate sin and call for repentance with compassion and care. Jude concludes by giving praise to God's power and glory, acknowledging his majesty, power, and authority through the Lord Jesus Christ, for all ages and generations.

Revelation

The book of Revelation is the final book and describes humanity's final hour. The Bible starts with Genesis revealing how humanity began, and the final book reveals how it ends. It describes the great white throne judgment, which is God's grand finale judgement of all the souls. It uses vivid symbols to show future prophecies. There are many references to these events throughout the Bible using key words such as the day of the lord, the great tribulation, day of wrath, birth pains, the last days, the final judgement, and the day of judgement. There will be key figures such as the ancient serpent or dragon which is Satan. Then Satan gives authority to the beast who deceives the world. There will be a false prophet God who works side by side the beast, he performs miracles claiming to be of God. Seven churches are judged. There is two witnesses from God, seven angels and trumpets, seven bowls, the second coming of Jesus who triumphs over evil, the great white throne judgement, and a new heaven and new earth. John receives a vision of these future events in the last days, everything will be made new.

In chapter 1, it starts with a prologue. It is a revelation from Jesus Christ, which God gave him to show his servants what must soon take place. God made it known by sending his angel to his servant John, who testifies to everything he saw. Blessed is the one who reads aloud the words of this prophecy, and blessed are those who hear it and take to heart what is written in it, because the time is near. The lord will come from the clouds, and every eye will see him, even the ones who pierced him. John acknowledges Jesus as the beginning and the end, the alpha and the omega. John was shown this revelation when he was exiled to a Greek island called Patmos. He was there in spirit when he saw the last days, a hand was put on his shoulder and was told to not be afraid because God is the first and the last. He heard a loud trumpet and was told to write on a scroll about the things he saw to send it to the churches. He uses metaphors, analogies, and extensive symbolism to describe what he saw. He saw seven golden lampstands and among the lampstands was someone like a son of man, dressed in a robe reaching down to his feet and with a golden sash around his chest. The hair on his head was white like snow, eyes were like a blazing fire, his feet bronze glowing in a furnace, and the sounds of rushing waters. His right hand holding seven stars with a double-edged sword coming out of his mouth, and his face was like the sun shining in all its brilliance. He is told that the seven stars represent angels, and the seven lampstands represent churches, then he is told that these events will take place in the end. God declares he is the living one, but death could not hold him because he holds the keys to death and is alive forever and ever.

In chapters 2, John is speaking to the seven churches, or the "lampstands." These are likely representative of all churches of all ages. They must live righteously and persevere in faith, turning away from complacency. It is a reminder that the road to spiritual growth and salvation is filled with trials and struggle. Believers are encouraged to stand firm with the guidance of Christ. The first church he speaks to is the church in Ephesus, who he gives credit to for their ability to call out false teachers and endurance during hardships, but they have become complacent in the love they once had. He tells them to consider how far they have fallen, to repent, and go back to the love and devotion they once had. The next church he writes to is the church in Smyrna, who were facing heavy persecution and poverty. John tells them these words are from the lord himself to comfort them during tribulation. He encourages them to remain faithful, even to the point of death or imprisonment. He says some people say they are Jews, but they are slanderers from the synagogue of Satan. He assures them to not be afraid of the suffering because Christ promises the crown of life to those who overcome. Next is the church in Pergamum, who is given credit for their steadfast faith in a city where Satan resides. But they are criticized for their tolerance of evil teachings of Balaam, which ended up leading others to sin. Others were enticed to sexual immorality and eating foods that were sacrificed to idols. He calls for them to repent, promising a hidden reward and a white stone to those who overcome. Next is the church of Thyatira, which is given credit for their deeds, love, faith, service, perseverance, and spiritual growth. But they are criticized for tolerating that wicked woman who claims to be a prophet and misleads God's children into sexual immorality and false idolatry. God gave her time to repent but she is unwilling, so those who commit adultery with her will suffer intensely unless they repent. God know the hearts and minds of everyone and has authority over all nations, those who keep their faith and does God's will until the end will be rewarded.

In chapter 3, God continues to judge the churches of the world. The church of Sardis has a reputation of being alive but are dead spiritually. God knows everyone's deeds and souls; they are called to wake up and strengthen what remains before it dies. They are called to hold onto the things they heard and repent because their deeds are unfinished in the eyes of God. No one knows when the time will come, so be ready because it will come like a thief in the night. Whoever has ears, let them hear what the spirit says to the churches. To the church in Philadelphia, they receive praise without criticism. God knows their deeds, they have kept Jesus' commands, never denying his holy name despite having little strength left. Since they have endured so patiently, they are promised to be kept from the hour of trial that will come upon the whole world. The lying followers of the synagogue of Satan will fall down to their knees acknowledging God's love for them. There will be a new Jerusalem, which is coming down out of heaven and Christ's new name will by written on the pillar of the temple. The last church is the church of Laodicea, who is criticized for their lukewarm faith. They are neither hot nor cold, lukewarm Christians will be spit out of Christ's mouth for their lack of conviction. They acquired wealth and claim not to need anything, but fail to realize they are wretched, poor, blind, and naked. True wealth comes from faith in Christ and righteousness. God calls them to be earnest and repent. Those who persevere are given the promise of sitting with Christ on his throne.

In chapter 4, after describing the lord's message to the seven churches in chapters two and three, John describes the end times events to come. He sees a door open in heaven and hears a voice like a trumpet speaking to him, the voice says, "come up here, and I will show you what must take place after this." He goes through the door in spirit and finds himself in the presence of God's throne. God appears to him in the likeness of precious jewels, representing divine symbolism, majesty, and authority. God had the appearance of jasper and ruby; a rainbow that flashed like an emerald encircled the throne. Jasper color representing purity and perfection and red representing God as the redeemer. Surrounding the throne were twenty-four other thrones, and seated on them were twenty-four elders. They were dressed in white and had crowns of gold on their heads. From the throne came flashes of lightning, rumblings, and thunder. In front of the throne, seven lamps were blazing. These are the seven spirits of God. He saw four living creatures around God's throne. He describes them being covered in eyes, both front and back. A lion, an ox, a face of a man, and a flying eagle. Each of the four living creatures had six wings that were covered with eyes all around, even under its wings. They are always watching the throne and praising the holy almighty God who always was, and always will be. The twenty-four elders lay down their crowns before the glorious, honorable, powerful lord and God who created all things.

In chapter 5, it reveals the locked away sealed scroll and the sacrificial lamb. John sees a scroll in the right hand of God, sealed with seven seals. A mighty voice asks who is worthy to break the seals and open the scroll. John weeps because no one in heaven or on earth is worthy to open it or even look inside. Then one of the elders tells him to stop weeping because the lion of the tribe of Judah, root of David has triumphed and been found worthy to open the scroll and its seven seals. Then he saw a Lamb, looking as if it had been slain, standing at the center of the throne, encircled by the four living creatures and the elders. The Lamb had seven horns and seven eyes, which are the seven spirits of God sent out into all the earth. He went and took the scroll from the right hand of him who sat on the throne. When he had taken it, the four living creatures and the twenty-four elders fell down before the lamb. They sing a new song praising the one who is worthy to take the scroll and open its seals. He was slain to redeem the world, and by his blood he saved all people from all nations. John witnesses a multitude of angels, numbering thousands upon thousands, joining in the worship. They exclaim in a loud voice the Lamb's worthiness, every creature in heaven and on earth give praise and honor to the God of glory and power.

In chapter 6, the slain lamb opens the seven seals, and each corresponding set of sevens reveal the next. John sees the lamb open the first of the seven seals and a white horse holding a bow appeared before him, he was wearing a crown, and he rode out as a conqueror bent on conquest. When he opened the second seal, a fiery red horse with a large sword came out, who was given the power to take peace from the earth and to make people kill each other. When he lamb opened the third seal, he heard the third living creature say, "Come!" he looked, and there before him was a black horse, and its rider was holding a pair of scales in his hand. He heard one of the four living creatures talking about food and days wages, signifying famine and war that inflate the prices of supply and demand, showing that people will struggle just to meet basic survival needs. Then the lamb opened the fourth seal, and a pale horse appeared before him, its riders name was death and was given power over a fourth of the earth to kill and destroy by sword, famine, and plague. When the fifth seal was opened, he saw an altar of all the souls who had been killed for spreading the word of God and their testimonies. They cry out asking the lord how long until their blood is avenged and the inhabitants of earth are judged. Then each of them was given a white robe, and they were told to wait a little longer until the full number of their fellow servants are reached, who will also be killed in God's holy name. The opening of the sixth seal leads to cosmic disturbances such as a great earthquake, the sun turns black, the moon turns blood red, stars fall, figs. These disturbances cause people to flee, kings, generals, rich, poor, the mighty, and everyone else start to hide. Unfortunately nobody can hide from the great day of judgement, they recognize God's authority and still refuse to repent because their darkened hearts are too far gone. They call out for the caves they hide in to fall in on them rather than face wrath of God.

In chapter 7, John sees four angels standing at the four corners of the earth, holding back judgement of earth until they put a seal on the foreheads of 144,000 servants of the living God. The angel says to spare the land, sea, and trees until these saved servants are confirmed. God uses them as vessels to spread the gospel and truth of God. John describes seeing a multitude of people in white robes from every nation, tribe, and language standing before the throne of God. They were holding palm branches in their hands and cried out in a loud voice saying that salvation belongs to God. The four living creatures and the elders fell down to their faces and worshiped God. These are the ones who have come out of the great tribulation; they have washed their robes and made them white in the blood of the lamb. For the lamb at the center of the throne will be their shepherd, there will be no more hunger, thirst, scorching heat, or suffering. God will wipe away every tear from their eyes.

In chapter 8, the seventh seal is opened which triggers the next set of seven trumpets. When he opened the seventh seal, there was silence in heaven for about half an hour. Seven angels stand before God, each given a trumpet. There is a high-ranking angel with a golden censor who came and stood at the altar. He was given much incense to offer, with the prayers of all God's people. The smoke of the incense, together with the prayers of God's people, went up before God from the angel's hand. The angel then fills the censer with fire from the altar and hurls it onto the earth, resulting in thunder, lightning, and an earthquake. This triggers the transition from seals to trumpets, seven angels had the seven trumpets prepared to sound them. The first angel sounded his trumpet, and there came hail and fire mixed with blood, and it was hurled down on the earth. A third of the earth was burned up, a third of the trees were burned up, and all the green grass was burned up. The second trumpet causes a blast of destruction to be thrown into the sea which causes a third of the oceans it to turn blood red, killing a third of sea creatures, and destroying a third of ships. The third trumpet causes a blazing star named wormwood to cause catastrophic destruction to the rivers and springs, making a third of the waters bitter and poisonous, causing many to die. The fourth trumpet causes a third of the sun, moon, and stars to become dark, causing naturally occurring light to plunge into darkness. An eagle in the sky proclaims the coming of the next three angels and trumpets.

In chapter 9, it continues with the angels and trumpets. The fifth angel sounded his trumpet, and the shaft of abyss opens up where dark forces dwell. When he opened the Abyss, smoke rose from it like the smoke from a gigantic furnace. The sun and sky is darkened by the smoke from the abyss. Out of the smoke emerges locusts led by a destroyer angel named Abaddon in Hebrew, or Apollyon in Greek. They were told not to harm the greenery of earth, but only those people who did not have the seal of God on their foreheads. They were not allowed to kill them but only to torture them for five months, the agony is like being stung by a scorpion. During those days, the agony will be so intense they wish they were dead, but they will not be capable to kill themselves. These locusts are the size of horses, have teeth like a lion, tails with stingers on them, and their faces are creepy resembling human faces. The sixth angel sounded the sixth trumpet, which triggers four demons to be released who are bound at the great river Euphrates. They have been kept ready for this moment and will kill a third of mankind. John hears the number of their army is twice ten thousand times ten thousand, which can be interpreted as an army of two hundred million. These horses and riders had breastplates that were fiery red, dark blue, and yellow as sulfur. The power of the horses was in their mouths and in their tails; their tails were like snakes, having heads with which they inflict injury. A third of mankind was killed by the three plagues of fire, smoke, and sulfur that came out of their mouths. Despite all this happening, some people on earth still refuse to repent. They did not stop worshiping demons and false idols, and never repent for their murders, magic arts, theft, or their sexual immorality.

In chapter 10, describes an intense moment of reflection about the mystery of God before the seventh trumpet. Despite the trials and tribulations faced, God will fulfill his divine promises made to the prophets and establish a new kingdom of righteousness. John sees a mighty angel descending from heaven, robed in a cloud and a rainbow above his head. His face was like the sun, and his feet like pillars of fire. The angel is holding a little scroll that is open in his hand, with one foot on the sea and the other foot on the land. He gave a shout like a roar of a lion which causes the seven thunders to speak. When John was about to write it down, the voice told him to seal it up and not write it down. This angel raises his hand to heaven and swears by the creator of all things that there will be no more delay. In the days when the seventh angel is about to sound his trumpet, the mystery of God will be accomplished, just as he announced to his servants the prophets. A voice from heaven instructs John to take the little scroll from the angel's hand and eat it, which makes his stomach sour, but his mouth is sweet as honey. John is told that he must prophesy again about many peoples, nations, languages, and kings.

In chapter 11, it reveals God's divine plan unfolding. These passages can be interpreted in different ways, but there are multiple references to a three-and-a-half-year timeline. It describes the temple of God, and the two witnesses who are killed and resurrected. The two witnesses clothed in sackcloth will prophesy for twelve hundred and sixty days, which is three and a half years. John is instructed to measure the temple of God and altar, with its worshippers. He is instructed not to measure the outside courts because it is reserved for gentiles, who will trample the holy city for forty-two months. The witnesses are referred to as two lampstands and two olive trees. Zechariah prophesied that, "these are the two anointed ones who stand by the lord of the whole earth." If anyone tries to harm them they will die, fire comes from their mouths and devours their enemies. These two will have great power to control weather and strike earth with plagues as often as they want. When the witnesses finish their testimony, the beast from the abyss kills them, and their bodies lie in the public square of the great city for three and a half days. The inhabitants of the earth from every tribe language and nation will gaze upon their bodies refusing burial, they will gloat over them and will celebrate because of the torment these two prophets caused on earth. But after the three and a half days the breath of life from God entered them, and they stood on their feet, and terror struck those who saw them. They ascend to heaven while enemies watch. At that very hour there was a severe earthquake and a tenth of the city collapsed. Seven thousand people were killed in the earthquake, and the survivors were terrified and gave glory to the God of heaven. This is the second woe of judgement, with the third coming soon. The seventh angel sounded his trumpet and loud voices in heaven proclaim the establishment of God's kingdom who will reign forever. The twenty-four elders in heaven worship God, acknowledging his reign. The nations are angry that God's wrath has come, the time of judgement of the dead and living has come. Then God's temple in heaven was opened revealing the ark of the covenant, and there were flashes of lightning, rumblings, peals of thunder, an earthquake, and a great hailstorm.

In chapter 12, is about the woman and the dragon. The crown of twelve stars represent the completeness of God's authority. A woman clothed in the sun is God's people and the son Jesus. The seven headed ten horned dragon represents Satan. John sees the war in heaven and the dragons pursuit of evil. A great sign appeared in heaven, a woman clothed with the sun, with the moon under her feet and a crown of twelve stars on her head. She was pregnant and cried out in pain as she was about to give birth. Then another sign appeared in heaven, an enormous red dragon with seven heads and ten horns and seven crowns on its heads. The dragon stood in front of the woman about to give birth so he could devour the child the moment he was born. She gave birth to a son who rules all nations with an iron rod, the child is snatched up to God and to his throne. The woman fled to the wilderness where she will be protected. War broke out in heaven. Michael and his angels fought against the dragon, and the dragon and his angels fought back. Satan was not strong enough, and they lost their place in heaven. The great dragon was hurled down, and that ancient serpent called the devil, or Satan, leads the whole world astray was hurled to the earth, and his angels with him. Heaven rejoices but a warning is given to the earth because the devil is filled with fury knowing his time is short. The dragon constantly pursues the woman, but she is protected by God, placed in the wilderness out of reach from the serpent. The dragon then goes off to make war against the rest of the woman's offspring, who are the ones who keeps God's command and hold to the testimony of Jesus.

In chapter 13, two beast are revealed, the beast out of the sea and the beast of the earth. The beast out of the sea is a figure who will reach world domination with him as the head shot caller, Satan will anoint him and his throne, giving him great authority over the world. He is represented to have seven heads and ten crowns on its horns, each head a blasphemous name. The beast he saw resembled a leopard, but had feet like those of a bear and a mouth like that of a lion. One of the heads of the beast seemed to have had a fatal wound, but the fatal wound had been healed. The whole world was filled with wonder and followed the beast. People worshiped both the beast of the sea and Satan since Satan had given authority to the beast. They look at the beast as if he is unstoppable and ask, "who can wage war against him?" This beast has a mouth that utters proud words and blasphemes. He will rule the world for forty-two months, or three and a half years. He opens his mouth to blaspheme and slander God's holy name, and also slanders those who dwell in heaven. He has the power to wage war against God's holy people and to conquer them, given authority over every tribe, people, language and nation. All inhabitants of the earth will worship the beast. The beast enslaves people who oppose him and kills many who refuse to bow down to him. God's people are called to endure and remain faithful. Next comes the beast out of the earth, this will be a false prophet. He performs great signs and wonders in front of the world. He confirms the beast of the sea as a legitimate ruler and people believe this false prophet because of the miracles he performs. The false prophet exercised all the authority of the first beast on its behalf, and made the earth and its inhabitants worship the first beast, whose fatal wound had been healed. He even caused fire to come down from heaven to earth in full view of the world. Because of the signs, he was given power to perform on behalf of the first beast, he deceives the whole earth. Because of the signs, it ordered the people to set up an image of the beast to worship. The second beast had the power to give breath to the image of the first beast, so that this image could speak and make sure everybody worshipped it. All who refuses to worship the image is to be killed. It also forced all people, great and small, rich and poor, free and slave, to receive a mark on their right hands or on their foreheads, so that they could not buy or sell unless they had the mark, which is the name of the beast or the number of its name. It will be difficult to function in society without the ability to buy or sell, so many people will be deceived and take the mark. That number is six hundred sixty-six.

In chapter 14, it shows John's visions of judgement, redemption, and wrath. Jesus is accompanied with his 144,000 faithful servants standing on Mount Zion, who have the Father's name written on their foreheads. These faithful believers sing a new song by the throne before the four living creatures and the elders. They are virgins who have not defiled themselves with woman, they never told a lie, are blameless, and follow the lamb wherever he goes. Three angels appear, each with a different message. The first angel proclaims and preaches the gospel to all the living on earth. The second angel announces the fall of Babylon the great, symbolizing the downfall of sinful world systems. The third angel warns those who receive the mark of the beast on their foreheads or hand, they are encouraged to remain faithful to Jesus because if they take the mark they will taste the wine of God's fury. The third angel calls on believers to be patient and endure, keeping God's commands. There will be no rest and there will be torment forever for anyone who worships the beast and its image. The son of man harvests the earth, representing divine judgement. The time to reap has come, for the harvest of the earth is ripe. Angels also participate in the judgement, comparing humans to cluster of grapes and a winepress. The angel swung his sickle on the earth, gathered its grapes and threw them into the great winepress of God's wrath, and blood flowed out of the press.

In chapter 15, John sees seven angels with seven plagues. This marks the completion of the seven trumpets transitioning into the seven bowls. There will be seven more plagues on earth. He sees a sea of glass with fire, symbolizing those who had been victorious over the beast and its image, and over the number of its name. They held harps given to them by God, singing the song of Moses and the lamb, praising God's greatness, righteousness, and holiness. They prophesy that all nations will come to worship God because his divine acts are revealed. John sees the opening of the heavenly temple, which is the tabernacle of the covenant law. Out of the temple came the seven angels with the seven plagues. They were dressed in clean, shining linen and wore golden sashes around their chests. Then one of the four living creatures handed seven golden bowls to the seven angels. Then the temple was filled with smoke from the glory of God and from his power, and no one could enter the temple until the seven plagues of the seven angels were completed.

In chapter 16, God's wrath continues with the seven bowls. A loud voice from the temple told the seven angels the time has come to pour out the seven bowls. The first angel went out and poured his bowl on the land, bringing painful sores to those who carry the mark of the beast and worshipped its image. The second angel poured out his bowl on the sea, and it turned into blood like that of a dead person, and every living thing in the sea died. The third angel poured out his bowl on the rivers and springs of water, and they became blood. The angel in charge of the waters tells God that he is always just in these judgements, as the holy one, God cannot do anything wrong or sinful. God is justly punishing the wicked murderers by giving them blood to drink, which represent the consequences of their actions, specifically the shedding of the blood of God's holy people and prophets. The fourth angel poured out his bowl on the sun, and the sun scorched people with fire. They were seared by the intense heat but still refused to repent or glorify God, cursing his name. The fifth angel poured out his bowl on the throne of the beast, and its kingdom was plunged into darkness. People gnawed at their tongues in agony cursing God's name because of their pains and sores, still refusing to repent for the things they had done. The sixth angel pours his bowl which dries up the Euphrates river, preparing the way for the kings of the east.

Then three impure spirits that look like frogs emerge from the mouth of Satan the dragon, the beast of the sea, and the false prophet, gathering for the great battle. They are demonic spirits that perform signs, and they go out to the kings of the whole world, to gather them for the battle on the great day of God Almighty. In Hebrew, the place is called Armageddon. Blessed are the believers who are alert and ready when the day of the lord comes. Paul mentions in Thessalonians that it will come like a thief in the night unexpectedly, so it is best to stay awake and not be shamefully exposed at that time. The seventh angel poured out his bowl into the air and a loud voice from the throne declared that it is done, bringing the last days into its final stages. A massive earthquake occurs bigger than any quake in mankind's history. Then came flashes of lightning and hailstones weighing a hundred pounds. The people continue to curse

God because the hail and plagues are so terrible and devastating. Cities worldwide collapse into rubble, and the world systems will fall, just like Babylon.

In chapter 17, John sees a great prostitute who is referred to as the whore of Babylon. This chapter uses different symbolic imagery to describes these days. One of the seven angels tells John to follow them, to show him this great prostitute who sits by many waters. The kings of the earth commit adultery with her, and the inhabitants of the earth were intoxicated with the wine of her adulteries. Then the angel carried him away in the spirit into a wilderness. There he saw a woman sitting on a scarlet beast that was covered with blasphemous names and had seven heads and ten horns. The woman sitting on a scarlet beast symbolizes powerful, corrupt religious and political systems, characterized by idolatry and moral corruption. The scarlet beast symbolizes support system for this immorality. The color scarlet symbolizes sin, blood, and violence. These religious and political powers influence and maintain its authority through force and persecutions. This woman is drunk on power and blood of God's holy people, the blood of those who bore testimony to Jesus. This astonished John, the angel said it will explain the mystery of the woman and of the beast she rides, which has the seven heads and ten horns. This beast is an entity that will arise out of the abyss of the depths of evil, this entity was once a powerful force that will arise again to go to its destruction.

The ten horns represent ten kings who have not yet received a kingdom but will gain authority with the beast temporarily. The seven heads represent seven hills on which the woman sits. They are also seven kings, five have fallen, one is, the other has not yet come but when he does it will only be temporarily. This beast is an eighth king; he belongs to the seven and will eventually reach his destruction. This scenario describes where ten kings who are powerful political entities, they will unite and give their power to this evil beast, signifying a moment where various world leaders will align themselves with a single, dominating force, potentially signifying a time of great political and religious consolidation under one oppressive world leader. Essentially, they will willingly surrender their authority to this evil power. They have one purpose and that is to give their power and authority to the beast. United, they wage war against the lamb, but the lamb will triumph over them because he is lord of lords and king of kings. The lord will have his chosen and faithful followers behind him. The angel tells John the waters and prostitute woman he saw symbolize peoples and nations that have been seduced away from true faith. The beast and the ten horns will turn on the prostitute, strip, and devour her. The woman he saw is the great city that rules over the kings of the earth. God is the ultimate judge, and a lot of people and world leaders will be handed over to the beast until God's words are fulfilled.

In chapter 18, it is about the downfall of Babylon, a reference to the sinful and immoral world governments of the last days. Worldly kingdoms and economies built on sin and greed is coming to an end. God is giving a last call for people to separate themselves from the corrupted world and repent. John sees another angel coming down from heaven who had great authority, the earth was illuminated by his splendor. With a mighty voice he shouted "Fallen! Fallen is Babylon the Great! She has become a dwelling for demons and a haunt for every impure spirit." All the nations have drunk the wine of her adulteries, and the merchants of the earth grew rich from her excessive luxuries. A voice from heaven gives a warning to escape Babylon's judgement, so they will not share in her sins anymore or receive her plagues. All her sins have piled up and God remembers her crimes. She will be paid back double for her crimes. She glorified herself boastfully and lived in luxury, she will get as much torment and grief to match her pride and self-importance. She placed herself like a queen saying she will never mourn, but one day the plagues will overtake her with death, mourning, and famine. She will be consumed by fire, for mighty is the Lord God who judges her. All the kings of earth who also committed crimes with her will see her downfall, watching from a distance terrified at her torment. The businesspeople and corporations who gained their wealth from her will weep and mourn because nobody is buying their product anymore. They will say, "the fruit you longed for is gone from you" meaning all the luxury and splendor will vanish, never to be recovered. They will weep because of the consequences of prioritizing material gain over spiritual values. Babylon the great, which represents the powerful and corrupt system that embodies wealth, luxury, and immorality will be completely lost. All that wealth will disappear so fast it will leave people shook; they stand far off as they watch their livelihoods disappear in such a short amount of time. John hears the saints, prophets, and apostles rejoicing at destruction of evil forces. God has finally judged the corrupt and wicked, vindicating the faithful who have been persecuted. In the finality of Babylon's downfall, a mighty angel throws a large boulder into the sea, symbolizing the total destruction of Babylon. God's righteous judgement is coming to a close and all the world's most important and rich people will never be heard again. The satanic music industry, the political, economic, and governmental systems of the beast have reached total annihilation. The lights of Babylon will never shine again. No more people being led astray by magic spells. In her was found the blood of prophets and of God's holy people, of all who have been slaughtered on the earth.

In chapter 19, many voices praise God for his righteous judgments and great victory over evil. These events mark the end of the tribulation and the long-awaited return of Jesus on the white horse. There is a roar of people in heaven shouting hallelujah, salvation, glory, and power belonging to God. He condemned the great prostitute who corrupted the earth and avenged the blood of his servants. The twenty-four elders and the four living creatures fell down to worship God on the throne crying hallelujah and amen. There will be a wedding of the lamb and his bride, the lamb being Jesus and the bride being his faithful believers. This is a symbolic representation of the union between Jesus Christ and his followers, where the redeemed will be united with Christ. The bride has prepared herself and given fine linen to wear, representing the righteous acts of God's holy people. The angel tells John to write down that blessed are those who are invited to the wedding supper of the lamb, and added that these are the true words of God. John falls to his feet to worship the angel but the angel tells him not to do that because they are also fellow servants of the lord, same with all the brothers and sisters who hold the testimony of Jesus. John is told worship God alone because all true prophecy is about Jesus and his ministry.

John saw heaven standing open and there before him was a white horse, whose rider is called faithful and true. The white horse symbolizes victory and purity. Faithful and true symbolizes his faithfulness to his promises and true to his word. With justice he judges and wages war, signifying his role as both judge and warrior against evil. Jesus returns with his eyes blazing fire, and on his head are many crowns with a name written on him that no one knows but he himself. The crowns represent his dominion and authority over all, ruling over all creation. His eyes of flame show his ability to see through all deception and evil. The name written on him signifies his holy nature beyond human comprehension. He is dressed in a robe dipped in blood, and his name is the word of God. Out of his mouth is a sharp sword with the ability to strike down nations and his robe says king of kings and lord of lords. John sees an angel standing in the sun, who calls all the birds to the great supper of God to feast on the flesh of the fallen. Kings, generals, the mighty, the beast and its armies gathered together to wage war against the rider on the horse and his army, but the beast was captured and so was the false prophet who performed signs on its behalf. These two had been responsible for leading many into sin, fooling those who had received the mark of the beast and worshipped its image. The two of them were thrown alive into the fiery lake of burning sulfur. The rest were killed with the sword coming out of the mouth of the rider on the horse.

In chapter 20, it describes Satan being locked away and bound for a thousand years while Christ reigns for those thousand years, it also describes the final judgement of Satan and the dead. John sees an angel coming down from heaven, holding a great chain and the key to the abyss. He seized the dragon, that ancient serpent who is the devil, and bound him for a thousand years. He threw him into the abyss, locking and sealing it over him, so he could not deceive the nations anymore until the thousand years ended. After that, he must be set free for a brief time. John sees all the souls of those who had been martyred and beheaded because of their testimony about Jesus and because of the word of God. They did not worship the beast or its image and did not receive its mark on their foreheads or their hands. They came to life and reigned with Christ a thousand years, which is called the first resurrection. These martyrs are blessed and holy getting a reward in the first resurrection, the second death has no power over them, and they will be priests of God and of Christ. The rest of the dead do not come to life until the thousand years end.

Then Satan faces judgement, he will be released from prison when the thousand years are over. He goes out and deceives the nations again in the four corners of earth, gathering them for battle. The army that rebels against God's people will be massive, with their numbers being as large as the sand on the seashore, representing a large-scale attempt to ruin God's divine plans before his final judgement. Evil and humans still rebel against God even after a period of peace and righteousness. Satan and his army surround the camp of God's people and the city he loves, but fire came down from heaven and devoured them. The devil, the great deceiver was thrown into the lake of burning sulfur, where the beast and the false prophet had been thrown. They will be tormented day and night for ever and ever. The judgement of the dead has come and there is a great white throne, where both righteous and wicked will stand before God and be judged according to their deeds. John sees the dead, great and small, standing before the throne and the books open, which represent a record of people's actions used to determine their fate. The dead were judged according to what they had done, as recorded in the books. Everyone will be held accountable for their life choices and face the consequences before God. Another book was opened, which is the book of life. The book of life is a list of names who will live forever in the kingdom of God. Death and Hades were thrown into the lake of fire, which is the second death. Anyone whose name was not found written in the book of life was thrown into the lake of fire.

In chapter 21, it paints a picture of the new heaven and new earth, it describes the new Jerusalem and the bride of the lamb. John sees the new heaven and earth which had no sea, the former heaven and earth had passed away. He sees the holy city and the new Jerusalem coming out of heaven from God, prepared like a bride beautifully dressed for her husband, symbolizing the intimate relationship between Christ and his church. God's dwelling place is now among the people, they will be his people, and God himself will be with them and be their God. He will wipe every tear from their eyes and there will be no more death, for the old order of things has passed away. God, who is seated on the throne, proclaims that he is making everything new and tells John to write down these words because they are trustworthy and true. He says to John that it is done; he is the alpha and the omega, the beginning and the end. God will give water to the thirsty without cost from the spring of the water of life. Those who are victorious will inherit all this; he will be their God, and they will be his children. The cowardly, the unbelieving, the vile, the murderers, the sexually immoral, those who practice magic arts, the idolaters, and all liars will be sent to the fiery lake of burning sulfur. This is the second death. One of the seven angels who had the seven bowls full of the seven last plagues came and told John to come so he could show him the new Jerusalem. The angel carried John away in the spirit to a mountain great and high, and showed him the holy city, Jerusalem, coming down out of heaven from God. It shone with the glory of God, and its brilliance was like that of a very precious jewel, like a jasper, clear as crystal.

The city is described in detail, including its great high wall with twelve gates and twelve angels at the gates, with three gates in each direction. The wall of the city had twelve foundations, and on them were the names of the twelve apostles of the lamb. The angel had a measuring rod that was made of gold to measure the cities walls and gates. It gives the exact dimensions of the buildings. The wall was made of jasper, and the city of pure gold, as pure as glass. The foundations of the city walls were decorated with every kind of precious stone. The first foundation was jasper, the second sapphire, the third agate, the fourth emerald, the fifth onyx, the sixth ruby, the seventh chrysolite, the eighth beryl, the ninth topaz, the tenth turquoise, the eleventh jacinth, and the twelfth amethyst. The twelve gates were twelve pearls; each gate made of a single pearl. The great street of the city is made of gold, as pure as transparent glass. There is no temple in the city because the Lord God Almighty and the lamb are its temple. The city does not need the sun or the moon to shine on it because the glory of God gives it light. Its gates will never be shut. Nothing impure will ever enter it, nor will anyone who does what is shameful or deceitful, but only those whose names are written in the lamb's book of life. The glory and honor of the nations will be brought into it, and God's holy people will live in a state of eternal peace.

In chapter 22, it describes the beauty of the new Jerusalem, comparing it to the garden of Eden. The angel shows John the river of the water of life, which was as clear as crystal, and flows from the throne of God and of the lamb down the middle of the great street of the city. The tree of life stood on each side of the river, bearing crops of fruit, the leaves of the tree are for the healing of the nations. There will no longer be any curse. The throne of God and of the lamb will be in the city, who will see his face, and his name will be on their foreheads. There is no longer any need for light because God is light, and they will reign for ever and ever. John is told that the lord is coming soon, and blessed are the ones who keep the prophecy of this scroll. The angel affirms these words are trustworthy and true, the lord who inspires sent this angel to show his servants the things that must take place soon. The time is near for the prophecies of this scroll, so let the holy person continue to be holy. God will give each person what is due according to what they have done. Blessed are those who wash their robes, they have the right to the tree of life and may go through the gates into the city. Outside are the dogs, those who practice magic arts, the sexually immoral, the murderers, the idolaters and everyone who loves and practices falsehood. Jesus, who is the root and the offspring of David, and the bright morning star sent his angel to give them this testimony for the churches. The spirit and the bride is a free gift, let those who come to Christ drink the water of life freely. It gives a strict warning to those who alter or take words away from this prophecy, God will add to that person the plagues described in this scroll.

They will not share in the tree of life and holy city described in this scroll. Those who testify that the lord is coming soon, may the grace of the Lord Jesus be with them, Amen.

www.ingramcontent.com/pod-product-compliance
Lightning Source LLC
Chambersburg PA
CBHW050455110426
42743CB00017B/3367